# steps to hap_ _ _ss

travelling from depression and addiction
to the buddhist path

by taranatha

windhorse publications

Published by
Windhorse Publications Ltd
11 Park Road
Birmingham
B13 8AB
United Kingdom

Cover image: 'Hiking Boots, Canteen and Map' © Royalty-Free/Corbis
Cover design: Marlene Eltschig
Printed by Cromwell Press Ltd, Trowbridge, England
Photographs between pages 92 and 93 are from the private collection of
the author

*A catalogue record for this book is available from the British Library*
ISBN-10: 1 899579 63 X
ISBN-13: 978 1 899579 63 1

# contents

introduction                            1

the turning point                       3

kawau island                            9

depression                             12

limbo                                  20

death ... and life                     22

recovery                               32

childhood                              36

boarding school                        45

university                             50

career                                 54

becoming a family doctor               58

the family doctor                      64

treatment                              69

lighter moments                        72

death                                  77

finding the way                        89

the discovery of compassion            93

opening the heart                     100

alone                                 105

testing the water                     112

the family within                     116

subhuti and friendship                125

going forth                           129

the secret valley                     135

the return journey                    143

rivendell                             147

communities                           152

a buddhist in the city ...            158

... and in the bush                   169

growing old                           177

# introduction

Now that these pages of memories, reflections, and flights of imagination are written, what stirred me to start such a venture and to stick with it through so many hours of toil in a field that I had not thought my own? The suggestion to write it arose in 1991, in the course of a discussion with Subhuti, my principal Buddhist teacher. Having spent some time drawing me out on my experience, both personal and professional, of a number of medical matters, especially alcohol dependence and depression, he remarked, 'These things need to be more widely known. You should write a book.' This planted the seed that sprouted, over the next few years, into a bundle of notes and essays. The more I wrote, the more I discovered about my history, my conditioning, my motivation, and my identity.

At the same time, I was making progress on the Buddhist path. I discovered that each new understanding came to me not so much by written or spoken word as by the direct example of someone else's life and actions. Could my life be an example in the same way? If I recorded my experience and made it available, perhaps it could.

As far as possible, I have taken myself back to incidents and their accompanying states of mind, and written from within the events as they happened. The great variety of experiences recalled and recorded over several years might make for a bewildering inconsistency of style, and you might feel this to be the work of a family rather than a single author. In a sense you would be right. If you find that history sometimes mingles with disembodied states, mythical figures, and childlike fantasies, neither reject these accounts as fantastic nonsense nor revere them as spiritual revelation; they are simply experiences from different levels of awareness.

The result of all this effort is an account of the creation of a life, making the best use of the material I brought with me, together with all that I discovered along the way. Initially this process was mainly fortuitous, but with time and practice it became increasingly conscious and directed. Its writing has revealed a great deal to me. If you find it helpful or merely entertaining I shall be doubly rewarded.

I did not set out to write an autobiography, but to trace the sinuous course of my spiritual development. Large sections of my life, especially the intense involvement over thirty years with marriage, and five wonderful daughters who resulted from it, have received scant attention. I found I could not write freely about people I love, with whom I shared all the joys and inevitable tensions of family life, without causing them embarrassment, and thought it best to allow them their privacy.

Although I write under the name of Taranatha, through the early part of the book I refer to myself as Robin, the name given to me at birth.

# 1

# the turning point

There wasn't much to mark it as a turning point at the time. 22 September 1975: the spring equinox. I was sitting slumped in my usual wicker chair, looking over the Hauraki Gulf in the soft, evening light. The usual iron fist was clamped round the back of my neck – the result of another long day's consulting. The gin and vermouth by my side, the evening light glinting on the deeply cut crystal of the tumbler. All this was so normal.

The soft pinks and purples of the eastern sky in the dusk. Tiri Light, the brightest in the southern hemisphere, or so they said, sweeping past every thirty seconds, making me lower my eyes to avoid its glare. Two sails drifting lazily by. Had I ever seen the Gulf without a yacht or two somewhere in sight? Who were these people who sailed through the edges of my life year after year? Did they, too, have fists of steel clamped round the backs of their necks at the end of the day? Or were they as relaxed as their sails in the faint evening breeze?

On the eastern horizon the blue-grey bulk of Moehau Range, misty, indistinct, except for one sharp peak kept hanging, unsupported in the haze, by a ray of the dying sun. The islands, Tiri with its white lighthouse and white house huddled below. Did anybody live there now that the light was automated? 'The Noisies', losing their outlines in the fading light to become stark, black rocks set in the shining sea. Vague shapes on the horizon, Mount Hobson and the smaller peaks of Great Barrier, and a little further north the faint outline of the massive hump of Little Barrier rising from the sea. Further still to the north, the silhouette of Whangaparaoa Peninsula, the sharp lines of its cliffs contrasting with the shaggy skyline where a row of old pines rose above the horizon.

Tui claiming its territory in the hibiscus at the end of the terrace. What an astonishing range of notes, from the harsh, rasping chuckle, through octaves of fluid notes until its voice disappeared beyond human range. Sunk in my chair, I watched the single white feather on the bird's throat dancing with the effort of its song, while to my ear, nothing – silence interspersed with occasional tiny sounds at the extreme range of my hearing. How many years had this tui been claiming this territory? Other familiar birds – the blackbird in his accustomed totara tree by the pond, shouting defiance at who would violate his space; behind it all, a chorus of less familiar bird voices from the surrounding scrub. And always the sound of the sea, now the gentle plop and splash of lazy ripples stroking the beach, at other times the crash and roar of wild waves beating themselves on the cliff.

Very ordinary things happening. I had come from the surgery as usual, poured myself the usual gin and vermouth, and flopped in the usual chair. Finishing both bottles at the same time was very unusual. I had automatically reached in the cupboard for replacements, and found none. Though it was very odd, there was no surprise; I hadn't reacted with the expected panic when I found my supply was exhausted. There seemed an inevitability about the sequence of events leading up to the last drink, but this time, somehow, it didn't seem to matter. This was unheard-of.

I sat watching the colours fade in the darkening sky, lost in the view over the Gulf that I had enjoyed for fifteen years. Vaguely aware that I should be more concerned about those empty bottles. Not easy to replenish stock at this time of the evening. A passing thought from nowhere in particular. 'If I didn't buy any more gin, that would change things.' It would indeed. It would change fifteen years of progressive alcoholism that I had accepted, with characteristic resignation, would kill me. There was no need to face the alcoholic death, slow, miserable, undignified. I would hang on until the last of the children didn't need me any more, then I would arrange an accident that would allow the insurance to be paid. This was a vaguely grim comfort, to know that I could take control of my own death, but not to allow myself to think too deeply about it. Carefully hidden thoughts – revenge for all that I had suffered in my marriage, atonement for the guilt of letting myself become a common drunk, anger accumulated over a lifetime of giving to people who gave nothing in return – all to be wiped out at a stroke.

I had experienced so much in my forty-five years, suffered so much, learned so many skills that I could give to the world. I had driven myself so hard, and all that the world could do was suck me dry. Yet I knew that underneath it all I was worthless. Sooner or later these parasites who were sucking my blood would find out that what they were getting from me was a sham. What little acceptance they gave me would vanish as they left me for a real doctor, a real father, a real husband. I would never wait for that to happen. An 'accident' would square the accounts – all of them.

I had made no attempt to deny the disease, at least not to myself. What I had denied was the possibility of recovery. It just did not occur to me that I could recover and live without alcohol. Now there was an entirely new factor – stopping drinking. Why hadn't I thought of it before? Another thought best not looked at too closely. I knew very well why I hadn't allowed myself to think of it. To accept the possibility of recovery was to accept responsibility for action, beginning with giving up alcohol. A whole new world was opening, a world free from the tyranny of alcohol, a world of clarity, of fearful freedom, a world whose existence had never until this instant entered my mind.

What would it be like not to wake each morning with the sick fear that today may be The Day They Find Out, when my world would collapse round my head? (Was yesterday The Day They Found Out? I don't remember all of it. Could they be wondering at the office how to tell me that they know, that the pretence is over, and my disgrace is exposed to the world?) Not to struggle with slurred speech and fuddled mind trying to hide my shame. Not to fear each traffic officer, knowing that I was over the limit. Not to plan the working day to avoid operating until the morning tremor had settled enough to allow me to place a fine stitch. Not to.... So many possibilities. So many freedoms. Such fear of the black hole that would open each evening as I didn't take the first drink. And the headache. What to do about that if there weren't the first gin of the evening to dissolve it?

I watched with detached interest as these thoughts chased round my mind. I did not realize – I could not have known that evening so many years ago – the momentous importance of what was happening.

A glance back over my forty-five years. Childhood in the hills of Taranaki, boarding school, medical school, and the post-graduate years in London. Marriage, children, and suburban general practice in Auckland. Each step following the last on a conventional, respectable path. No real decisions made. No conscious options seen. I was riding the river of fortune, accepting no responsibility for the direction or speed of travel. But behind the façade the sinister shadow of alcohol growing ever darker. For fifteen years I had been clinging to the raft on the racing river of circumstance as it lurched towards disaster. And now, this evening in early spring, that rush had stopped. Just like that.

No obvious decision even now – it seemed to be just another link in the chain of events that was my life.

If I was scarcely aware that this was the first real rebellion against the forces that had carried me so far, I was even less conscious of the process I was starting. The first firm 'No' to passive acquiescence to the destructive flow. The first 'Yes' to Life. The first glimmer of understanding that my life was my own, to mould as I would, to enjoy, to build as high as I wished.

The elation of the following morning as I faced my new life – and *nobody knew there was anything different*. Externally, there was nothing different. I normally started on the day's gin in the early evening – until then it was business as usual. In fact, even I had no idea that this was the first day of a complete change in life's direction. But with the sunset there were problems to be met. What to do with the hand that usually held the glass? And how to manage the aching in the throat that craved the feel of raw gin? A small substitution – lemon juice. And lemon juice it was for the next few weeks. I must have drunk every lemon in Castor Bay. The novel feeling of bright consciousness demanding a focus. There was certainly no lack of subject matter. Ysabel, my wife, despised money, and in my fuddled state I had been unable to manage the family accounts. So night after night I sat at the dining table surrounded by piles of papers, exulting in my mastery of planning and arithmetic.

As the chaos died down, the truth of the changes began to penetrate the family. Ysabel, at first congratulatory, soon became resentful of my new-found independence. So long adapted to my benign presence in the evening living room, she now found herself sharing with a whirlwind, and worse, a whirlwind that went its own way. I was beginning to question the old order, to propose changes, even to take the initiative in some small things like the work and mealtime routines.

Memories of the next eighteen months have a shiny hardness about them, as of glass or marble. Activity, efficiency, achievement. Wilful drive without the relief of the soft, blurred evenings. Triumphant energy and aggressive health. But the coffers were being drained. I knew the drinking had been symptomatic. I knew too that it had become a disease in itself, producing its own symptoms. But stopping drinking relieved only the symptoms of the addiction. Even in this stage of embryonic understanding of dependency disease, I knew there were powerful forces driving me to drink, and that, taking no steps to meet this part of the syndrome, I was far from cured. Hence the wilfulness behind the drive to efficiency. Hence the inevitable collapse.

When it came, in the autumn of 1977, it was nothing as crude as a relapse. On a cold, clear Saturday morning I was hunched in my parka on the sidelines of a netball court as a daughter's team met a tough adversary in that game of speed, skill, and close team work. A thump in the middle of the chest, and another, followed by a whole series. Overwhelming *angor animi* – that sense of impending disaster associated with disturbances of heart rhythm. The trained clinical observer took over. Runs of extrasystoles on a background of sinus rhythm with normal sinus arrhythmia. Not a heart problem. So, how was I feeling? That broke through the defences that had prevented my asking myself that question for months. I was feeling absolutely nothing, no pain or joy, no happiness, anger, or even fear. My life was flat and grey. No wish to do anything, just the drive of a tyrannical will. I was severely depressed, and had been becoming so for months.

'If you were half as impaired by tuberculosis or an injury as you are now by depression,' Tony, my friendly psychiatric colleague, insisted a few days later, 'you wouldn't dream of trying to go on working. You would accept that you are sick, and it's OK to be sick, and take time off to recover.' That sort of soft talk was all part of the act. I had responsibilities to meet. My next final year student was about to join the practice for a month. (For many years I'd had three or four students in the practice every year.) On-going problems with patients to sort out. If I were to accept that I was seriously ill, it would mean a course of antidepressants and six weeks off work. Ridiculous! I had not taken more than two days off work in years. People needed me. So, propped up by the faintly protesting Tony, I struggled on, guiding the student as best I could. I have never seen that young man again, and I wonder what he thought of the strange month he spent with me. When he left he gave me tapes of the Sibelius and Tchaikovsky violin concertos, which are still favourites. Each walk from chair to door to admit the next patient demanded a new effort of will. Sometimes I felt, 'I just can't do it. I can't open that door to another demand on my resources. The bucket is empty. There is no more to give.' But there was always a little more.

As the student left, thinking his own thoughts, I was back in Tony's office. I had crossed the next four weeks off my appointment book, and demanded to start full doses of antidepressants. To hell with the side-effects. I had no time to pussy-foot about with slowly increasing doses to minimize the dry mouth and constipation, and the spaced-out feeling and the rest of the misery of starting these drugs. And I was going to the beach cottage at Kawau Island to be by myself and recover. Poor Tony did his best. 'If one of your patients said he was going to an island by himself to start a course of antidepressants, what would you tell him?'

'I would tell him that in about two weeks, when he starts to recover, he could be a serious suicide risk, and shouldn't be by himself.'

I can still hear his insistent words. 'In about two weeks, when you start to recover, you could be a serious suicide risk. You shouldn't be by yourself. I don't think it's very clever.'

I didn't give a damn what he thought. I took my box of drugs and a supply of food that needed no preparation – I knew I would have no motivation to cook – told the family I needed a rest, and went to the seclusion of the island. I didn't tell Ysabel about the drug, or the suicide risk, although I suspect she was aware of both.

# 2

# kawau island

The cottage on the island had been part of the life of the family for five or six years. For ten years before that, we had been renting a nearby cottage in the same bay for family holidays. Gillian and Alison, the eldest of our brood, had spent their summer holidays there from pre-school days. Each of the children in turn had played naked on the beach, staggered and splashed in the shallows, learned to swim, then to row *Small*, the tiny dinghy that had started my boat-building career. Each had learned to sail one small boat or another in the succession of small boats I had built or otherwise acquired over the course of the years. All had caught fish, built huts in the bush, taken increasingly ambitious walks through uncharted bush, and marked their routes on the big map on the wall. As the family boat made its appearance, then grew in size and power with the years, each was towed round the bay on a piece of plywood, a surfboard, an outsized inner tube, on water skis, and, with the latest and fastest boat, two together, each on one ski. A succession of school friends had stayed there, sharing all the things that can be shared in such an idyllic place. The boat shed had become a dormitory, its walls decorated with posters and murals of cartoon characters dancing their way between the studs.

For me, Kawau was the sea and boats, the bush, and long exploratory walks – and a chance to step cautiously outside my doctor role and be part of the family. In fact, with a marriage based on mutual dependence, and the all-pervading father role, my family persona was not much different from that of the office. For all of us, Kawau meant family sharing in a setting of peace and beauty. In our island life there was a semblance of communication, sadly lacking at home, and therefore all the more precious. This was the natural place for me to come to start my life, or to end it. Here was a haven for the wounded soul, a safe cave for the mortally stricken to die in solitude, or a birthing bed for a new life to endure the tortures of rebirth.

Memories crowded in. Two small girls of about six, one of ours and a visitor, failing to return from a walk. Anxious roamings and searchings, whistle-blowing and shouting, until a faint cry replied from far below. They weren't worried – just hungry. A 5-year-old and friend suddenly missing, together with *Small*. Frantic racing round the bay in the family boat, until the tiny boat and two little heads were spotted over a kilometre away and still rowing. An indignant child's voice, 'But, Daddy, you said *Small* was good enough to row to Mansion House,' in answer to my scolding. And so I had said jokingly to a neighbour who had jeered at such a miniature example of the boat-builder's art. Mansion House was the Governor's residence, now a museum, all of three kilometres away over open water.

Sleeping, surrounded by children, under the stars, and being woken by a sudden downpour. Sleepy children stumbling over wet sleeping bags, finding their way in the dark to shelter. Building the new water tank, helped by 16-year-old Gillian, and Phillip, the first of a series of boyfriends to move into the family ... beach bonfires and moonlight swims ... wallabies scampering off into the bush as we passed ... Susan's fall from a rope swing, losing her grip while swinging wide over a steep hillside on a rope hung from a tall pohutukawa tree. A double break of the right forearm and a nightmare journey in a neighbour's launch through heavy seas. My back to the cabin wall, feet pushing against the bunk opposite, and the injured child enveloped in arms that felt every twinge of her pain. The rest of that summer taking turns with Ysabel and the older children carrying Susan's plaster while she swam in the sparkling sea.... Gillian falling while carrying a small sister over the oyster-covered rocks. Her pain and remorse as the child howled her indignation, blood running down her face from a row of scratches.... My sunset excursions, sometimes alone, sometimes with children, to catch fish for breakfast, and the feasts of fresh fillets the next morning. I was appreciated. 'Nobody cooks fish like you,' they said so many times....

Memories tumbling over each other as the ghosts of the children crowded round in the evening gloom of that solitary cottage. Around me the familiar things – the walking map that Ysabel and the children had made, the woven flax mats, cowrie and bristle-urchin shells, and the jar of sloughed cicada skins. The tide chart on the wall above the cupboard of wet-weather games. Books, magazines, children's stories shouting their memories of stories read, cuddled together in bunks and makeshift beds. The box of gumboots by the door, under the rack of raincoats and sun-hats. The row of sea urchin shells, carefully graded by size, on the window sill.

As a backdrop, overshadowing each new scene, the spectre of alcoholism, of gin bottles hidden in the basement, of efforts to hide slurred speech and fuddled thoughts from Ysabel and children, and the knowledge that when these idyllic scenes had passed, my life would end in my death in disgrace.

# 3

# depression

How long I sat in the crowd of silent, reproachful ghosts I have no way of knowing. They came from a world of sunshine and colour, where there had been a living father and husband. Now they relived their past, noticing with scorn, if they noticed at all, the shell of the man they thought they had known.

At some time during that first night alone I roused myself to turn on a light. The room was empty, cold, silent, the blackness of the windows reflecting my heart's lack of hope. But there were decisions to make, action to take.

The boat was moored, all gear stowed away, and the cover buttoned down. Food was stored, the water supply attended to, and the cottage prepared for occupation – the same routine I had followed every time I had visited here over the years. I was free to have a good look at myself. I was alone and without responsibilities for four weeks. What Ysabel had told the children about my going away I did not know, nor did I care. She was quite capable of managing the family without me. Perhaps the least inaccessible of my deeply buried emotions was resentment at Ysabel, which may have explained my satisfaction at having left her to manage alone. For the children I felt only a strong sense of duty. But my value to them was only as a provider. They would be better without me. I couldn't provide anything more for them than a home and a cheque book, and the insurance would deal with that. They had picked a bad one for a father, which was their misfortune, over which I had no control.

The box of antidepressants – hundreds of capsules of Imipramine – lay in the centre of the dining table. I could swallow the lot, which would be much the easiest course. But that would invalidate the insurance. I may have been a useless drunk and a write-off as a father, but I was not going to walk out on my responsibility to the girls. Gillian was OK – she was to be married in a few months. Alison was about to move into a student flat. I had nothing useful to offer her. Margaret seemed happy enough at high school. Susan was having some problems at school, but Susan had always had problems, and I was no help to her. Eight-year-old Liz stirred a slight response, soon replaced by pity, then hatred towards me. A little girl making her way in life with a useless, depressed drunk for a father, and probably the added burden of his suicide to deal with. It was not fair that she should have been landed with this sort of fate. Could it be worth the effort of trying to recover, to make some sort of human being of myself? But the pain, and the work, and the hopelessness. What prospect of any sort of success? And so on. I knew through all this that I would start taking Imipramine according to the schedule Tony had written, and would stay alive while waiting for signs of recovery. I knew I hadn't the power to decide to do anything else.

Time to reflect on what I knew about depressive illness. So much that I had read and heard from the many people who had reported their experience to me. My mind raced, searching through all this useless knowledge. What people commonly called depression was just a transient state of low mood, loss of enthusiasm, difficulty with decisions, and the world becoming colourless and hostile.

I could have been writing a textbook or lecturing to medical students. 'Spontaneity is lost, every action takes great effort for so little result, nothing is fun any more. Even food and sex become drab and uninteresting, although some people grasp at one or other in a frantic effort to get some satisfaction. Sleep is broken, and dreams are hectic. But there is feeling, often too much feeling, since so much of it is negative. There is fear, anxiety, anger, resentment, and guilt. Yet with all this emotion, there is inactivity – what I call 'paralysed indecision'. Essentially, emotions are in conflict. So much energy is expended in the battle that there is not much left to power the rest of life. Behind the apparent passive inactivity there is a turmoil of frantic indecision. Attention is limited, flitting from one activity to another – taking up a book and putting it down with half a page barely read, starting to wash the dishes and leaving them to make a phone call, deciding with hand on phone that it is too difficult – perhaps later – and so on. Until the whole process gives up, and nothing is done at all. So the days pass, with gales of motive power blowing now this way, now that – perhaps from all directions at once. And there is weeping. Tears of frustration, of self-pity, of pity for the world (in the midst of personal misery the world's misery can become unbearable), and tears of plain, undiluted unhappiness.

Fortunately, this painful state is usually self-limiting. The common name of 'reactive depression' gives the clue. Among the many conditions giving rise to this state of mind there is often one major, and transient, one, the passing of which allows equanimity to be restored. Restored at least to the level at which it was before, unless the episode is used, as it could be by the more aware, as a source of learning and progress. But there are dangers. The frustration of being buffeted by conflicting motives, added to the sheer exhaustion of disturbed sleep, can be just too much to tolerate. If the only relief is the oblivion of death, that can be what is chosen. And although decision-making is difficult, there is still emotional energy enough for it to happen. The conflicting winds need to align themselves for only a few moments to produce strong, decisive action – which can be death.

All this had only the most superficial resemblance to the state of mind that was threatening my life that night at Kawau Island. This was the dark state that was in the old textbooks called 'melancholia'. If I could accept the existence of 'diseases', then this was undoubtedly one – a stereotyped pattern of symptoms and signs that I had heard described in the same flat voice by so many people in the past. This was no emotional turmoil; this was dark despair, hopelessness beyond all hope of hope, a scarcely living death whose horror was that it was not death. Awareness was very much alive – thoughts rolling on in ceaseless ruminations of despair. But conscious emotion was dead. There was not only no optimism, enthusiasm, or enjoyment; there was no anger, fear, or even interest. Nothing touched the heart to rouse a response. The nearest approximation to emotional awareness was the ruminating activity of guilt and resentment.

Yet I knew that, for all the appalling greyness, what I was suffering was not as painful as the more superficial variety that my academic mind had been running on about. Conscious feeling, including awareness of pain, was at such a rudimentary level. Like a deep burn that destroys the pain receptors, my deep depression produced numb insensitivity.

Still the teacher's mind rolled on. First to go, so the books said, was usually sexual interest. That's how it was for me. Not only had the fading embers of sexual desire in my unsatisfactory marriage cooled to ashes; there was no flicker of response to any of the myriad blatant sexual images spread round the city by the advertisers. This loss of interest, I reflected, could well be atavistic. It was not appropriate for populations to breed in times of famine or stress. How often could I remember a remark about loss of 'the urge' being a pointer to depressive illness lurking behind a shield of more acceptable symptoms.

However, people told me that sexual performance, once interest was aroused, could remain intact until many other functions had departed. I had no grounds from which to confirm or deny this fascinating observation, but I knew that in reactive depression, added anxiety often led to impotence, which could in fact overshadow the loss of libido. So frustration would grow on misery.

Then other symptoms developed, pointing to the essential problem, which was blanket loss of emotive power. All of this I could see had been happening to me. Attention would not stay where it was asked to be. Reading anything that required concentration became impossible. Even holding a conversation was difficult. Thought devoid of emotion functioned only as thought, but ground to a halt when faced with the need for action. Decisions went from difficult to impossible. A picture in memory of a depressed patient standing in a supermarket, hand poised before jars of jam, paralysed by the inability to choose between strawberry and blackcurrant. Only a week or two earlier I changed my socks twice while dressing, because I couldn't decide between grey and white. Eating became a chore, buying and preparing food a nightmare. Every act required effort of will. In the absence of available motive power, natural, spontaneous activity just faded out, sometimes stopping completely for minutes or hours. This was the well-known picture of the melancholic, blank-faced and immobile, staring into space with dumb, unseeing eyes. Even involuntary activity faded out from time to time, the previously willing bowel becoming as reluctant as other activity.

Now that I was safely removed from the need to do anything, or to try to look normal, I was able to reflect further on the strange state in which I found myself. It all tallied so closely with the textbook descriptions, and the accounts I had heard from other sufferers, that I found myself, almost against my will, becoming interested. What had happened was a profound loss of motive. This I could understand, but what I had not realized was that this included loss of physical endurance. Muscles, I found, would respond only to a limited extent to wilfulness. I had heard tell of hills becoming towering mountains, and stairs growing steeper and higher. Now I knew that the path from the jetty to the cottage was no longer a gentle slope, but a precipitous climb, once made, not to be taken on again without great thought. The horse being flogged, if not quite dead, was becoming so insensitive as to be indifferent to the whip.

15

With such profound changes in my whole being, it was hardly surprising that my circadian rhythm, the built-in timer that rules the daily cycle of activity, should be thrown out of kilter. Again, I was following the characteristic pattern, falling into an exhausted sleep soon after lying down, only to wake after two or three hours. Fitful sleep often returned, but with the dawn came the lowest point of the cycle. The day ahead was dull, dark, grey, and, if invested with any feeling at all, fearful. Life ahead was a succession of dull, dark, grey days, linked by nights of even more active despair. As the day ground on, the mood would often lift a little, which explained my recent tendency to arrange the more difficult appointments towards the late afternoon.

I was not given at this stage to wonder much about the causes of this dreadful condition. But I did think, as I do now, that there was a lot to investigate in such a catastrophic disturbance in well-being, and then, as now, I shelved it for a future date – if there were to be one. But even in that state I could not but be intrigued by the mechanism of the present illness, and the possible effects of the chemicals piled on the table. If the drug were to be effective, it had to be because it promoted something that was deficient, or suppressed something that was overactive. In some way it had to push the distorted biochemistry towards normality. I had no doubt that there was a physical dysfunction behind all this. It felt so solid, so concrete, that it had to have a basis in 'matter'. As I reflected, the picture came to mind of a depleted reserve of fuel for the emotional centres of the brain. If I had been driving the mechanism beyond its capacity to produce fuel – if the starving system had gleaned the last grains of sustenance from the reserve stores – this would produce something like the present situation. The organism was being driven by thought alone. It was almost as if the support departments had gone on strike, and the administrators from head office were slaving in unfamiliar territory to keep at least a semblance of normal function going. Now that it was accepted that the system could stop to restore itself, activity had ground to a halt. The main engines had stopped, and the auxiliaries had been driven beyond capacity.

This analogy of excess of demand over supply of chemical fuel was in fact not very far from the truth – which left me, theoretically, with clear alternatives – use less, or supply more. But using less was no longer an option. That implied overall reduction of stress, not only to a 'normal' level, but far enough below normal to allow restoration. I was at this stage in no shape to sort through the mechanics of stress.

This could wait to a later stage, but – if I survived – I would have this fascinating topic by the tail in due course. The only thing I had changed in my recent life was my alcohol intake. All the stresses that had led to the alcoholic state had been thrust aside, hidden behind a screen of wilful activity. Although stopping drinking had solved my most immediate problems, it had at the same time removed my first line of defence. I was now threatened by facing myself with clear perception, robbed of the blurring and softening of outlines that alcohol had provided. Added to that was the fact that I was unwell – in fact seriously, dangerously, ill – which doubled a burden already too heavy to lift. I had long since lost the ability to make decisions. This was no time to begin facing the major changes required to reverse the imbalance.

Now the catch-22 was becoming obvious. A year or more ago, when the symptoms first began to develop, before decisiveness was seriously damaged, I could perhaps have begun the strip-down and refit my life needed. But I was at that stage not suffering enough to want to tear down the edifice of my old life and rebuild. By the time the seriousness of the problems began to show I was no longer capable of action. (Many years later I discovered the teaching of *dukkha*, the essentially unsatisfactory nature of life, which I was surprised to recognize as an old friend. It is only when awareness of unsatisfactoriness is strong enough to overcome attachment to the present that growth takes place.)

Having disposed of the possibility of reducing the demand, I was left with no alternative but to supply more of what was needed. Now I was back in biomedical territory. If a system is out of balance, give it a good push to straighten it up. In purely mechanical terms, this is fine. But unfortunately nature is not purely mechanical, and is given to pushing back if one leans on it. If the sensitive, dynamic balances of nature are to be influenced – if I want to correct an imbalance – it behoves me to be deeply aware of the nature not only of the system involved, but also of the imbalance. Aware, too, of the likely response of the system to my intervention, and of the effect on other systems, near and far, their effect on one another, and so on. All too often in my medical past I had been wilfully ignorant of all of this, wielding a club when a rapier would have been appropriate, and a rapier in place of a soothing touch.

However, to return to my dilemma. I had given the pharmacology of depressive illness some study. There was plenty of material available, since there was big money in the supply of relevant drugs. The first difficulty was that antidepressants would not cure depression. Very rarely could a medicine be said to cure anything. The best the physician's art and science could do was to change some conditions, alter the dynamic balance of a process, to favour movement towards harmony. Wherever this process started, be it in the realm of structure, mechanical function, chemistry, or psychology, the object was the same – the move towards total harmony of the individual within their own being and as an aspect of the cosmos. Such was the innate drive of all beings towards completeness that a fumbling push, provided it was in the right place and the right direction, might be all that was needed to establish health. This, I reflected, was fortunate, because as I reviewed my life in medicine I could see that a great deal of what I had done, apparently successfully, had been of this order.

But back to my ruminations of life and death – my life and death – in that island cottage. Pharmacology is rarely a matter of pouring a carefully measured quantity of the missing chemical into the right place to correct a defect. The antidepressant I was planning to use was certainly effective – so effective that Tony had been heard to say, 'Depression is that which is cured by antidepressants.' But its action could hardly be described as precise. It appeared to be a base chemical from which the body could manufacture its own supply of what it needed. But it took time; ten to twenty days before any result would be felt. Since each day was an eternity of black despair, surviving two or three weeks in this state was beyond imagining. Then there were the problems that the drug itself would bring. Drowsiness and a feeling of unreality, dry mouth, and constipation, to add to my misery. The bumps – heart rhythm upsets – would be worse. Trouble with close focus of vision. Fortunately, I had already decided that my arm was not long enough to reach my book, and I had invested in reading glasses. My body, already like a lump of putty, would feel even heavier and more reluctant to move.

As if all this weren't enough, I knew that 'antidepressant' didn't have much to do with depression. All the drug could do was kick the emotional centres of the brain into action, restoring some emotional power that I could then apply to my recovery. Even that had its black side. How often had I heard depressed patients in the early stages of recovery complaining of being riven by fear, anger, and guilt, as their new-found emotional awareness became caught up in these powerful negative states. Happily, but ineffectively, I would as physician assure these tortured people that this was a sign of returning life, and that within a few days they would be able to enjoy, to feel warmth and enthusiasm.

Round and round went these thoughts until half the night had passed. Then, exhausted, and devoid of the imagination to do anything else, I took my first dose of Imipramine, made my bed, and lay down.

# 4

# limbo

Memory of the next week or two is a strange jumble of pictures, connected only by their shared lack of clarity. Blurred pictures.... A fat, pink woman with an English accent emerging from the bush, lost while walking from a yacht moored in the next bay. Noting with detached surprise that my legs would carry me, slowly, halfway up the hill behind the cottage before refusing firmly to go any further. Hiding behind a flax bush as a stranger beached a dinghy and walked to the cottage. Spreading another slice of Vogel Bread with Marmite and adding a slice of cheese. I have no memory of eating anything but Vogel and cheese during that hazy time. Doing nothing, wanting nothing, thinking not very much. Sleeping ten or twelve hours a night, and some more in the afternoon. That was a strange property of Imipramine – restoring the ability to sleep without itself being truly sedative. I had plenty of lost sleep to make up.

After a week – or perhaps it was two – I began to notice the activity about me. The tui were excitedly claiming territories. I could not but be aware of their bulky steel-blue bodies and noisy, fluttering flight, their competitive calling from their favourite trees, and their aggressive display when their territory was invaded. But now I could hear the immense range of pitch and quality of their notes, and appreciate the courting displays, bodies glinting in the sun as the birds hovered and fluttered high above their chosen trees. Wekas, too, were active. These are flightless brown rails, as big as domestic hens, strutting with look-at-me importance, screaming and gurgling at each other in raucous conversation day and night. Wallabies, usually dawn and dusk feeders, were made bold by hunger and tempted into the full sun by the first growth of spring grass.

As I watched this activity I felt myself coming alive – alive to the pain of shame and worthlessness. It is strange to see with hindsight how completely my conceptual knowledge of the process and inner awareness were divorced. I knew that this phase of active, burning misery was temporary, that within a few days it would pass. But in my guts I knew that this was my true being. Whatever happier state I could find myself in at another time was a sham. I truly was worthless, a burden on family and society. Others might conjure up a display of effectiveness and even enjoyment. That sort of pretence was not for me. All I had to do was devise an accident that the insurance people wouldn't see through, and my troubles would be over.

Then, one showery morning, I noticed that the pine trees on the headland were singing their strong southwesterly song. The wind and the sea were rising, and although the beach faced the mainland only six kilometres away, quite powerful breakers were crashing on the shore. There had to be a way to drown in a stormy sea without rousing suspicion. A boating accident. But nobody would take a boat out in that sea unless there was an emergency, or unless they were already out there when the wind came up. Everybody knew I sailed the battered aluminium dinghy for long distances. I could have been out there an hour ago when conditions were good. But I would have to wear a life-jacket or they would know. Perhaps the old one with the rotten straps that I could break....

Slowly the plan emerged. I would sail the dinghy out to North Passage. Something was bound to break in that wind, and I would drown, especially if I lost my life-jacket with a broken belt. And – here was the beauty of the plan – if I lost my nerve when I was out there I couldn't change my mind. If I sailed a long way down wind there would be no chance of getting back, no possibility of having to come back to living. Life had been flat, grey, hopeless, not worth the effort. Now it was an agony of remorse and self-blame, but still with no hope of relief. No, I certainly did not want the chance to change my mind just because I might be a bit cold or frightened.

# 5

# death ... and life

*Be very deliberate. Concentrate, even if you have to beat your brains to do it. There must be no mistakes. The insurance must be paid. Put on all the usual gear – cloth hat, blue T-shirt and the old green pullover with the seagulls on it, the windbreaker, blue shorts, and boat shoes. The old life-jacket, and don't forget to break the belt. Leave the house just as you have left it every other time. Don't do that extra tidying. Don't turn off the electricity or the water. Don't lock up. This is an ordinary morning sail – nothing different. Don't let yourself think you aren't coming back – you'll do something silly. Don't hang about. Wind is coming up fast. Won't be long before the waves are roaring in on the beach so you can't get out to sea.*

Remember the days when you wouldn't face half of this wind, and you were younger and fitter then. What has happened to fear? Guess it has something to do with knowing I'm not going to go on living. After all, what could go wrong now? Perhaps I could fail to die.... But that's the worst, as long as I don't make the sort of silly mistake that could lose the insurance.

Poor, old *Bucket*, you battered old friend. It isn't fair to do this to you, after all we have enjoyed together. Making it look as if it is your fault. Remember the day we first sailed together? Oh God, that was so many years ago. The kids said boats weren't made of aluminium. 'Looks more like a bucket,' they said. Well, they all made good use of you.

That weak starboard chain-plate – two rivets gone and the third a bit loose. If I sail hard on starboard tack it will probably tear away, and that will look just right. If it doesn't, a bit of extra pressure with the foot should do it. I can't be weeping for you. Must be just the spray. I'm not weeping for myself. I won't. I won't. Might make me make that mistake.

*Follow the usual routine. Lift the mast against the wind. Shackle the forestay and shrouds, and tighten the pins. Just the sort of day a shackle pin could come out, and that wouldn't be healthy. Tighten the kicking strap – about as hard as it will go for these conditions. Come off it, man, you aren't out racing today. You don't really need the ideal sail shape for best speed. Run the sheet through the blocks and keep your mind on the job. Everybody knows you are meticulous about this routine, and something different would blow the whole plan. A bit tighter with that figure-of-eight knot. Losing the end of the sheet would be just the sort of stupid thing that would lose the children's insurance. Now up with the sail, and watch out for that flailing boom.*

Oh God, that sail is taking a hammering before we have even left the beach. Will it make it? Incredible noise it makes thrashing in the wind.

*Get the rudder on before you go in the water – you'll never manage it after – and hope you don't smash it in the surf.*

Down the beach on the old trolley. Clever bit of engineering – just a triangle of kanuka poles on wooden wheels and tyres from an old Mini. Very efficient, and rustproof. I wonder if anybody will ever use it again?

*Get your back to the breakers, drag the boat off and let the trolley find its own way home.*

So cold. I won't be able to keep concentration and hang on to the sheet and tiller if I get too cold. 'Get your wet weather gear on before you get wet and cold,' the book says. That guy should be out here to see how things really are in rough weather.

The next lull – heave myself over the side – and we're sailing. Centreboard down and tied in place. Tie the rudder hard down – it'll break if it is anything but vertical in this sea. Bum wedged on the gunwale, feet under the straps, and sheet in as far as I dare. What a noise the whitecaps make as they crash on the side of the boat. My next boat will be wood – aluminium is so noisy. My next boat.... But this is quite some wild ride. I could let myself enjoy it even if it is taking me to death. The elements aren't fighting me. There is some harmony here in this awful primitive power.

The crashing and flogging of the sail – the roaring rush of the waves, the crash and crunch of the hull hitting the next wave, and the splash of water slopping over the gunwale. The whipping, stinging spray on the face as the hull throws water high into the wind. The insistent ping-ping of the taught halyard slapping on the mast. The wild tugging of the tiller as each wave grabs the rudder. The challenging lurch of the hull with each renewed blast of wind. Salt water stinging in my eyes. Exhilaration, wild and joyful, joining forces with the elements of wind and water. Taking up the challenge with no fear – no feeling but the crazy delight of being part of all this – being welcomed by the sea and the wind. Accepted as part of this power, this energy, this life.

But I am not going to live. I am going to join these elements in my death. Let them swallow me, take me with them into new experience, away from the dreadful living death of numbness that is all the life I have known for so long. To live on this level for a moment is to welcome death – but not just yet.

Hang in there, *Bucket*. Enjoy this last wild ride with me. Hold together a bit longer, my dear old friend – let us go to a wonderful, glorious death together. Brace your shrouds to meet each gust. You can take more than this, and my love and skill are all with you.

Did I say love? What is love to discover among these awful elements? I haven't known love for so long. Hard, harsh, hateful – I haven't known love ever, not love of recognition, acceptance, being me, and that's OK. But now, my old friend, I begin to feel for you a deep, all conquering love, as for part of myself – the part that takes up the challenge of living at last, living a proud, wonderful moment in our ride together to join these elements in death.

No time to wonder if death is appropriate. This living is so new that I will drink it in great gulps even to death. Oh *Bucket*, my friend, you must be part of me to join this dance of death with such abandon, but such skill.

But we have work to do, you and I. I mustn't be seduced by all this noise and excitement. It is time we went about and did what we came for. Wait for it – the gap before the next gust. Now! Heave on the tiller, lurch across the boat, then – chaos! A shattering noise, and a flash of light. Now only blinding pain where my head was. Violent movement – I feel sick – noise of howling wind, water slopping over me. Oh God, that's the boom thrashing about over my head. It must have hit me. There's blood pouring down my face. Take it slowly. I'm on the bottom of the boat among oars, bailer, rope – it must be the end of the sheet – and a shoe floating in bloody water. We have rounded up into the wind. What in God's name am I doing here? I was going to die, but why? I don't have to die. I've never been so alive. I can get with that wild wind and water again and go on living.

*Bucket*, we're going home! You and me together – we're going home. It will take more than a gale to stop us. We are going to try to go home. Oh *Bucket*, your damaged chain-plate that was going to be my friend in death. How about it now that we're going home? One loose rivet where there should be three good ones. What a perfect set-up for an accident, and now I don't want one! And if it didn't tear out I was going to kick it out. Doesn't look as if it would have taken much of a kick. Keep the weight of the wind off it somehow. Sail on a reach with a loose sheet. Spill most of the wind until we are upwind of the beach, then gybe and sail mostly flat off on port gybe. We could get away with it, but nothing is lost if we don't. We came out here, you and me, to die, so that's OK. But, *Bucket*, I owe it to you, my old friend, to bring you home. I will bring you home – or die in the attempt. Ha, ha!

Enough of this! I must concentrate. If I get us through this sea it will be the biggest thing I've ever done.

*Easy on that chain-plate. The leech is flogging so hard it must tear into shreds. Keep some tension on the shroud so it doesn't jerk that rivet out. And keep bailing. This is no spray coming over the gunwale; this is green water in big lumps.*

It would be easier if the blood didn't keep running into my eyes. But there is plenty of sea to wash it out. I'm getting cold, so cold. I hope I don't get so hypothermic that I lose my judgement. It will take every bit of concentration I ever had. I'm tired, tired, tired. Is the pain exhaustion or cold? No matter.

*Don't look for the beach with every crest – it won't get any closer for a long, long time.*

The wind is still coming up. The troughs are deeper, but that's OK, I can't see how far I have to go from down there.

*Concentrate!*

*Sheet in a bit on each wave to bring the gunwale up. Ease off at the top or that rivet won't make it. You don't have to keep anything in reserve. You'll either be dead or you can rest for ever when you get home.*

So tired. Is it worth it? I could just give up and drown.

*The challenge, man, the challenge! Keep your mind on the job and hang in there. And don't get to thinking about that hot shower back at the cottage or you'll never make it.*

Oh God! That was a big one. One more like that and we'll be swamped.

*Bail out, man, fast, before the next one comes over.*

Strange how dead the left hand looks on the tiller. I could have been dead for some time by the look of that. If I drown I guess my whole body will look like that. Can't feel the right hand at all. I wonder if it will ever write, or put in a fine stitch again? But it must be OK – the sheet seems to be working by itself. Sail trim is good, very good. And it has to be – anything less is death. If I ever get this poor old wreck home I'll have learned a thing or two about heavy weather sailing. *Bucket*, old friend, you were never made for this.

*Easy on the tiller. Rudder stock is springing apart with each big one. Reckon it would be asking a bit much to get home without a rudder.*

The piece of manuka pole I poked in there when the tiller gave up so long ago is the strongest piece of equipment on the boat. Rudder will hang together, but the stock looks bad. I wonder how long it has been like that? I must check these things more carefully in future – if there is a future.

*Watch it! That sort of thinking will get you dead.*

'The prudent skipper looks right round the horizon at least every five minutes,' the book says. Well, what if you can't see over the next wave most of the time, and when you can, the blood gets in your eyes? What then, Mister Clever Master Mariner who writes the books in a warm, comfortable office somewhere in the city?

*Don't waste your anger, man. You need every bit of it to keep this boat going. You are letting too much water stay in the boat. It's heavy and unstable. Just do what has to be done, and concentrate! If you tip over now you'll never get up again. Don't waste all that effort and pain. Concentrate! Just too silly to drown now for want of a bit of effort.*

It all seems to be working, tiller, sheet, balance, bailing, and I'm not really aware of any of it any more.

*Well, you have to stay aware of it.*

Two sail battens gone, and a bit of a rip round the top batten pocket. I wonder if the sail will last the distance? The island can't be far away.

*Have a good look from the next crest.*

There it is, about straight down wind. Now, how to turn? If I gybe I may well go over, and there will be one hell of a jerk on the mast that could finish that chain-plate. If I try to go about I'll probably get in irons in this wind, and with so much water in the boat. But that's the best option, so here goes! 'Stand by to go about.' 'Aye, aye, captain!'

*Oh please, please keep your mind on the job!*

27

Sheet in carefully and point up a bit. In the next trough when we are shielded from the gale.... Now! Over with the tiller and watch that boom.... That's the end of that prank, in irons, driving backwards with water pouring over the tuck. One more wave like this and we're gone.

*Keep your head down and think – think how to get out of this. You're not dead yet.... Reverse the tiller and hold it till the stern comes round....*

Well, how about that? We're round and sailing again, and only half full of water.... Now we're driving nose-under. Over-powered with the full sail working and no chance of letting it off any further without bashing the boom on the weak shroud. Can't sail off on a reach – I'll never go about again. I can get a bit of weight off it if I sheet in a bit, but it's going to take a lot of power, and I haven't got much.

*So hang in there, get your weight back on the tuck, and bail hard.*

I don't think praying is going to do much. Even if there were a God up there, he would be getting a bit sick of me by now.

I'm going to make it. I'm really going to get home. There is still plenty to battle with, but *Bucket* is holding together and I'm keeping pace with the bailing. No chance of sheeting in to reduce effective sail area, but we're not taking in much over the bow. Roaring down the face of each wave. All I can do to stop broaching. Poor old *Bucket* was never meant to plane down ocean rollers. High time we got out of here – they'll start breaking if this wind gets up any more, and that I couldn't manage, not in this state of health. Beach gets closer with each wave that hurtles past. Strange feeling of going backwards as we fall off the back of each wave. Do waves go faster in a stronger wind, or just get bigger? Looks as if I'll live long enough to be interested in things like that.

This ride that began with a cold, calculated trip to extinction has become a fire of transformation. Life has burst out of death – life in its wildest, most ecstatic state. Alchemy – the transformation of death into birth. The god of transformation is Love. Strange that I should first have recognized this god in the form of you, *Bucket*, you unlovely aluminium hull with rough edges, clumsy and crude, but an extension of me. The part of me that carries intention into action. *Bucket*, you must have known that this ride could not have been to death. You must have known life would come out of these awful forces. Or did it take you by surprise too?

You and I became integrated in the experience. What do you mean to me? What unknown part of me were you?

You were responsive. In some strange way, you lovely, ugly piece of metal, you had a feeling that I didn't. You were the point of contact with life's forces. It was through you that I found the power of Life. You were so much more than a lump of metal – you were my sense organ and my way of contacting reality. Through you I found it, and through you I acted it out. We're going home together, you and I, and we're going to make it.

*Pull your mind back to the job – you're not there yet. Next big one is pulling the centreboard up. If it hits the bottom in a trough you'll roll over, and that wouldn't be good.*

If I get it up too early we'll probably tip over, which comes to much the same thing. Half full of water and flat off the wind, lurching and rolling like a sow in a wallow. Not at all sure I'm strong enough now to lift the board anyway. Don't bother about the rudder. It will probably survive, and if it doesn't I can make another. Up with the centreboard after the next wave. Get the strap undone – ready – heave – and again – it will catch the boom if it stays half up.

It's out, and I've lost it over the side.

*Forget it – it'll come ashore. You'll have to surf in on top of a wave – if you hit the beach in a trough the next one will give you a rough time.*

This is it! Thirty-five knots of wind in the sail and a great big roller underneath. Oh God, the beach is coming so fast.

Drop the sheet. Take a good grip on the tuck with the spare hand.... That was less of a bump than we took on most of the big, green ones out there.

*Don't hang about – there are more big ones coming behind....*

I'm above the bad stuff now. I can stop and rest....

*No, you don't, you'll freeze. Keep moving. Get the sail down and leave* Bucket *to the tide. No chance of shifting her up the beach.*

A hundred metres to the cottage. More like a hundred miles.

*Don't stop. Get your wet clothes off and warm up under the shower.*

I wonder if my body temperature is down. Skin looks soggy and quite dead. There will be a big load on my heart when the skin warms up. I wonder if I'm cold enough to be at risk for ventricular fibrillation? I'll never find a pulse. Guess I'll have to take a chance on that one. It would be a real joke if I dropped dead after making it this far.

*Keep moving – you're getting colder all the time with the wind in your wet clothes.*

Skin is numb. How am I going to know when the shower is tepid? Hotter would be dangerous. Feels either cold or burning.

*Shut up. Get under the shower and get your clothes off.*

Can't lift my arms. Shorts off first and sit down. Maybe it will be easier when I warm up a bit. It's going to hurt like hell when the skin circulation comes back. Last effort – soggy, bloody shirt and pullover off.

*Look at you! A bloody cadaver, that's what you look like.*

One thing is sure – if I were a cadaver I wouldn't hurt so much. How can a man be so tired and still live?

*Don't stop until you are wrapped in blankets and lying down.*

I need a hot drink, but I can't stand long enough to make it.

*Take some hot water from the tap. Wrap a towel round your head – it will stop bleeding soon.*

Good thing I didn't strip my bed. Was it this morning that I got out of this bed? It was a whole lifetime ago....

I woke to a brilliant sunset, orange and red clouds tossed with ever changing shape and colour over the hills of the mainland. To the north and east the delicate mauves and pinks of the darkening horizon. Sensations crowded in – exhilaration, fear, clear thought, pain in the head, sore, aching muscles all over, but it was all sensation, life. I was aware – I was alive! My scalp had stopped bleeding. Wonderful tissue for surgery – such a magnificent blood supply it would heal with little scarring whatever I did with it. So I did nothing, and the scar is indeed scarcely visible.

Slowly down to the beach. Poor abandoned *Bucket* was lying on her side, half buried in gravel. The tide had covered her and retreated while I slept. Injured, sore, and weary as I was, I could not leave her there to the mercy of the next tide. So as the last of the daylight faded, and the moon rose, I dug away the gravel, exposing her poor old body to the soft moonlight, just as I felt myself opening to the light of awareness. A final heave, and she was back on her trolley to the safety of the lawn.

Hunger – but no hurry. Savouring each new thought and feeling, I cooked my first proper meal since I had arrived and ate it by the light of the moon.

# 6

## recovery

Recovery had begun, and with it a narrowing of the gap between book learning and experience. I knew so well the two-steps-forward-and-slip-one-back progress, the saw-toothed graph typical of recovery from depression. The slip back into despair was the more painful because experience was now more intense and, hope having been felt, hopelessness was the more catastrophic. I sat long hours on the terrace during the next day or two, reflecting on these things and awaiting the inevitable bad day. Much of the time I made use of the enchanting track in the valley behind the cottage for these reflections. It was for years before and after these events the place in my life that led naturally to deep thought, to reflection, and in later years to meditation.

The crash was not long in coming. The sick dread in the belly as I woke a few days later under a solid, grey blanket of despair. 'This won't last. This is not what I am. Tomorrow I will feel better.' The litany repeated, over and over. But deep under all the busy reassurance, the knowing that the return of feeling, the glimpse of a future with effectiveness and even joy, was all a cruel trick of a sick mind. I would never be any good because I never had been any good, and that sort of change did not happen in real life. And so on, through a morning of misery. But it was misery with a difference. No longer flat and hopeless, it now had intervals of choking weeping surging into my throat like the belching, boiling mud of the Rotorua thermal pools. By evening it had given way once more to bright confidence peeping shyly through gaps in the grey curtain. So the days passed, periods of feeling alive growing longer and stronger, and relapses into depression, less shattering as I became more confident.

I could have guessed what the next stage would be. I seemed to be alive and well – what was I doing hiding on an island when there were patients needing attention and a living to earn? I don't remember how long it was – perhaps two or three weeks after that dramatic and dangerous demonstration in the boat – before I tidied the house, slipped the boat from its mooring, went home, and went back to work. Tony seemed pleased, almost surprised, to see me. Not much was said about my holiday, but now I knew I must set about sorting myself out. I was an alcoholic, albeit a dry one, and the proper place for alcoholics was with Alcoholics Anonymous.

As I feel my way back into state of mind when I first considered AA, I know that denial was still there – denial not that I had been addicted to alcohol, but that major changes were still needed to deal with the underlying dependency. It was easy for me to convince myself that I needed AA not for myself but for my alcoholic patients, so I picked up the phone as if to arrange another study course. Before I knew it I was caught in a new stream of events. John, whom I had known at university thirty years previously, and Don, whom I had met more recently, also turned out to be AA members. They promptly arranged to discuss AA with me – just for my professional education of course. Within half an hour I found myself telling (selected parts of) my story. I had to confess before the evening was through that AA was indeed for me. It was no use my protesting that, having been dry for two years, I did not need AA. I knew that was not true.

Unfamiliar and mostly unwelcome thoughts crowded in as I approached my first meeting. First humiliation, acknowledging that I needed help. Not only was I indeed a common drunk, I was about to confess it to a roomful of drunks most of whom would be way ahead of me on the road to recovery. Chatting in the privacy of an elegant home with John and Don, both well dressed, well spoken professional men whom I had met previously in 'normal' life, was traumatic enough; what I now faced was a crowd of strangers in the basement of an unknown church. In spite of John's assurance that St David's was the drawing room drunks' meeting, I had a picture in my mind of a gathering of unwashed, unshaven down-and-outs reeking of alcohol and cigarettes, taking advantage of the warm room and free cup of tea. And these were the people who would be first to see me as I was, stripped of all my old defences.

All too soon I found St David's Church, and John outside the door of its bleak basement. Yes it was a bit drab, and there were a few seedy-looking characters standing about, but even as I entered the room I knew this was home. John introduced me to Jenny, the cigar-smoking chairperson of the evening's meeting, and David, a corporate executive who was later to become something of a mentor, and many others who have since faded into anonymity. No fuss, just matter-of-fact acceptance of somebody whose only requirement for entry was that I wanted to be there.

Twenty or thirty people, mostly middle-aged, mostly, but not all, reasonably tidy, settling themselves on rows of unsympathetic chairs in a low-ceilinged room whose only decorations were Sunday school cut-out figures and drawings hung on strings across the room. Jenny sat on a small stage, 'Welcome, all. My name is Jenny and I'm an alcoholic.' So began six years of weekly meetings during which, encouraged by many men and women sharing their experiences with varying degrees of honesty and understanding, I was able more and more to share mine.

Before long I found myself reciting the twelve steps of the programme, reeling them off with as little concern and as little understanding as I had so many years before mumbled my way through the church litany:

(1) We admitted we were powerless over alcohol; that our lives had become unmanageable; (2) came to believe that a power greater than ourselves could restore us to sanity; (3) made a decision to turn our will and our lives over to God as we understood him; (4) made a searching and fearless moral inventory of ourselves; (5) admitted to God, to ourselves, and to another human being the exact nature of our faults; (6) were entirely ready to have God remove all these defects of character; (7) humbly asked him to remove our shortcomings; (8) made a list of all persons we had harmed and became willing to make amends to them all; (9) made direct amends to such people whenever possible, except when to do so would injure them or others; (10) continued to take personal inventory and when we were wrong promptly admitted it; (11) sought through prayer and meditation to improve our conscious contact with God as we understood him, praying only for knowledge of his will for us and the power to carry that out; (12) having had a spiritual awakening as a result of these steps, we tried to carry this message to alcoholics and to practise these principles in all our affairs.

But where the church litany had passed me by, the programme soon began to bite. OK, I didn't have control over alcohol, but *powerless*? Well, yes, I suppose I was powerless really. *Unmanageable*? No, I was managing my life well enough – if I didn't look too closely. And so on through the rest of the steps. The bit about God did not sit well until I realized there was a hierarchy of powers greater than me, beginning with the group of mutually supportive people I was meeting every week. I didn't have to name those powers if I didn't feel good about it. The big one was *taking personal inventory* and seeking to change and make amends; not matters to be cleared up before bed time or even by tomorrow, which was generally my approach to life.

With the passing months and years I found myself discovering, investigating, and to varying degrees resolving, the underlying causes of my alcoholism: a previously unacknowledged wish to depend on somebody or something, hidden anger and resentment projected on the world, perfectionism and the guilt arising from failure to meet impossible goals, and many more. As these demons great and small were lured from their lairs, named, tamed, and befriended, so their energies were diverted towards the growth of true independence and individuality.

Change breeds change. With the transformation of so many of my personal demons I was free to see more deeply into the philoso-phy of AA. It was not, as I had first supposed, an open-ended religion that would carry me as far as I wanted to go. It was a way for sick, even desperately sick, people to restore themselves to normal function, and there, at least for me, it stopped. Becoming less impaired I began to catch glimpses of a potential far beyond 'normal function'. Even-tually I felt I had outgrown AA, that it was all a bit simplistic, and that, having carried me as far as it could, it was becoming boring. It was time to resume the search for the spiritual path that, under the power of alcohol, I had abandoned some years before. It was time in fact to review my life to this point as a basis for seeking a way ahead.

# 7

# childhood

Mangamingi in the summer. Steep, broken hills, river flats smooth and green, streams, rivers, cliffs, and gorges. Sheep with bulky fleeces, red-and-white Hereford cattle, big men with rough voices, pack horses, riding horses, draft horses, and dogs, so many dogs. It was a land of brash, adolescent beauty. But in the background was the grimness of the struggle for survival.

A six-year-old trudging along a dusty road in bare feet – the cuckoo's call, magpies warbling, little clouds of dust rising from the toes. My father's dog whistle – especially that trilling call he used for Johnnie, the shaggy black-and-white huntaway. Len, the head shepherd, used to say he must be fed on canary seed.

Something sad and lonely about the boy dawdling and dragging his feet in the dust. Something a little fearful, too – demons in the clumps of bracken and the overgrown barberry hedges beside the road, even in the bright sunshine. Where was I going? To the wool shed. The racket of the shearing engine, clattering and echoing round the valley. The big flywheel that could fling a man through a wall or twist off his foot if he got it caught in the spokes. A fickle and dangerous monster, that engine obeyed nobody but Father, and even he was careful to approach it with due ceremony.

Shearers, big men dripping sweat as they worked, frightening me with the banter to which I didn't know how to reply. The fascination of the fleece falling away from the sheep's back in the long blow. The skill with which the big, clumsy handpiece found its way, so quick and delicate, round the forehead, eyes, and under the jaw. Such power and strength, moving with such grace.

I had left my mother in the house, always working – a tired look on her face. Was she loving? I don't know. She very rarely showed it, but how could she with all of her artistry and sensitivity squashed down like the springy fleeces in the wool press? What pressure she must have stacked up inside her, and what energy it must have taken to hold it there. Mother with the big meat cleaver cutting chops on a side of mutton for the shearers, the scrub-cutters, and for the family.

Baking and washing, housework, and soap making. Cooking gigantic meals for big men. Growing vegetables and preserving in rows and rows of glass jars, all boiled up in the enormous preserving pan. Did she smile or laugh? I am sure she did, but not often. She said she had no sense of humour, just a sense of the ridiculous. Yes, she was quick of wit and clever with words. And her Chopin, Scarlatti, and Beethoven flowed with such vigour from the old Marshall and Rose in the dark sitting room. At least to a child's judgement, it was music as it was meant to be. Though I never recognized it then, as I look back now I can see – and hear – all her anger and frustration howling from the piano, rocking on its castors to the *Military Polonaise*, *Appassionata Sonata*, and the like. The haunting sadness of the *Valse Triste*, and the soft, clear purity of the *Moonlight Sonata*.

It can't have been much of a life for Mother. Not much but the constant struggle for survival. From under the memories of constant work I do unearth moments of laughter and fun, even of playfulness – but not many. Mostly it was uncomplaining acceptance of her lot. Her relationship with me was something of a mystery. I was five when she went with Father to Nelson to take my oldest brother Geoff to boarding school. They went on for a rare holiday touring the west coast for two or three weeks, while I and my brother Ralph were left in the care of the resident maid – a neighbour's daughter who helped in the house – under the supervision of an elderly aunt who was spending an extended holiday in one of the farm cottages. 'They're back. They've come home!' called Aunt Sarah. Looking down from the cottage I watched with distant interest as the square-backed Austin pulled up at the front gate. It seemed no business of mine, but Aunt Sarah said, 'Go down and say hello to your mother.' So I went and stood in the middle of the dusty road while Mother, looking lost and uncertain, hesitated by the car. How we re-established contact after that moment of mutual bewilderment I don't remember. My memory is of total indifference, but the depth to which the incident etched itself on my mind suggests that conflicting forces were not far below the surface.

Fifty years were to pass before I learned about the beginnings of that relationship. Family tradition has it that for the first few months of my life the baby screamed. Just why the baby screamed nobody seemed to know. My thought from so many years later is that since I have inherited my father's hiatus hernia it is likely that the baby suffered the pain – not at that stage of medical knowledge a recognized condition – of gastric regurgitation. For whatever reason, it seems I effectively kept my exhausted mother from sleep until, against great resistance, she was persuaded to leave the children in the care of a nurse while she took a rest with an aunt in Auckland.

They must have been hard times for the family. Not long before I was born, Father had perforated a duodenal ulcer, which under the prevailing transport and surgery conditions should have killed him. I imagine he survived for the reason that he did so many heroic things: because it was his duty to those who depended on him. In the year of my birth, 1929, the Great Depression was barely past its worst. Hundreds of bales of wool were stacked in every shed. Prices at auction were less than the cost of transport. There was no money to employ help, but there was food and shelter, and people were pleased just to work for that.

What guided those dusty, bare feet to the wool shed? There I would find my father, deaf, soft spoken, commanding respect without ever raising his voice. Dad, for whom I worked, whose acceptance was the breath of life to me. For him I learned resourcefulness in making and mending, and in my artistry with a rifle. From him I learned to reject all that was not directly concerned with survival, all that was decorative or in any way superfluous. The fear of his disapproval, never demonstrated, hardly even spoken, governed my childhood.

How shall I tell of Father from so long ago? From my perspective he was tall, although in reality he was no more than five foot ten. Nearest to me, the farm boots, and dungarees held up by Domo police braces with the ends tucked through the tape loops carrying his woollen long johns. Grey checked shirt, tweed jacket, and battered felt hat. He never wore a belt like other men. He said it hurt his ulcer, so he carried a turnip watch in one trouser pocket and a pocket knife worn smooth by long handling, in the other. Other men, of course, carried a knife, and a watch in a leather case, on their belts. These distinctions gave rise to endless decisions. I usually carried a sheath knife displayed on my belt, as well as a pocket knife, to be safe in both worlds.

In his face, always smooth from the attention of an enormous cut-throat razor, a distant look. Somehow, even as a small child, I knew his thoughts were far away. The effort he made to hear me, to notice me, was often tangible. With more than the briefest pause in the conversation his attention would creep away to those distant places seen only by his grey-blue eyes. I see those eyes, from so many years later, shaded by bushy, white eyebrows, always focused on a distant vision. The reason may well have been as mundane as his explanation. 'One eye is for reading and the other for watching a dog working across the valley.' He certainly did read with one eye closed, and would sometimes work a distant dog with his hand over the reading eye.

Father's deafness was an accepted part of my childhood image. You had to talk in a special way if he was to hear – slow, clear, and a bit louder than normal. Of course you couldn't rely on it. Sometimes he would hear things not intended for him. You could never be quite sure if he heard or not. So there was no careless conversation. You had to get his attention first. Bring him back from wherever he was. Then the special voice – not using unnecessary words because each one was an effort for him. I became an expert at getting through to him. It was always worth while. That was what was different – he made the effort to hear me. He would often ponder my childish thoughts and give his considered opinion, which was always worth hearing. His world was his observation, his books – his evenings were spent deep in history or philosophy – and the thoughts that filled his private world. There was no place in that world for a mere child. When he took me into it I was received on his own level.

Only now do I begin to understand how it was that this remote and private man had such a profound effect on my life. It was in my brief journeys into his life that I felt accepted, recognized. How deeply I needed that acceptance is reflected in the completeness with which his values became my values. First, the total acceptance of the work ethic. Not to work for the security of your dependants (even if dependants were of the remote future) was unthinkable, sub-human. A cameo from about my eighth year: as we passed the front of the house together, Father pointed to the fretwork under the veranda roof. 'Just look at that, my boy. Think of all the useful things a man could have done in the hours that he spent doing that!' Personal needs were not put aside – they just did not exist in this world. Adversity was to be met with uncomplaining resignation. Success and good fortune became the property of the tribe, never to be claimed, as was the habit of more frivolous men, as personal reward. The origin of this ethic was not far to seek. My grandfather, a mythic figure long gone by the time of my birth, was one of the great Wesleyan lay preachers of the English Midlands of the latter half of Victoria's reign. Father had rejected God when he left home at the age of 16 to seek his fortune in the colonies, but the ethic was too deeply embedded to be cast off like a mere God. Where his other ethical values came from I never discovered, but the shock of discovering at an early age that they were flawed is still with me. While I was helping to pick peas in the farm vegetable garden, a turkey thrust an inquiring head through the hedge. Without a moment's hesitation Father took up a stick, smote the turkey smartly over the head and quickly stowed it in a sack, with, 'That will make a good dinner!'

It was the slightly furtive haste that made me question, 'But wasn't that Mr Brown's turkey?'

'Yes, but it got fat on our vegetables and now we'll get fat on it.'

Yet with all his burden of utility and duty, Father took pleasure in his fellow beings. There was the weekly game of auction bridge with Clarrie Nicholls, the schoolmaster, and Alice, his wife. Until long into the evening Father's chuckles would echo into my bedroom as he took, and usually got away with, the most outrageous risks in bidding. When he was younger, so I'm told, his hearing was less damaged, and he took delight in the rare chance for chat, or for deep conversation, with his fellow men. To some extent he reclaimed this part of his life when the first effective hearing aids became available. From this point he had a choice whether or not to be deaf. If there were angry or unkind words that he preferred not to hear, an almost imperceptible movement would remove him from the world of sound. Only those of us who knew him well could guess with any accuracy whether he was in contact or away in his own world.

However important was my father's approval, I needed approval too from the men, the farm workers, and from the few other children. My language was as filthy as any shepherd and his son, although I don't ever remember hearing Father swear, and Mother's worst was a 'damn' under her breath when she stumbled over a particularly difficult phrase in Chopin. So my life was divided in two by the back gate that separated the house and garden – the protected, controlled domain of family and cats, from the farm, the rough, dangerous domain of big coarse men with their horses and dogs. This double life persisted in one covert form or another until, many years later, it was welcomed into full consciousness as the division between the aesthetic-spiritual on one hand and the intellectual-practical on the other. Only then could these major parts of myself begin to work in harmony.

There were not many important people in the life of a back-country child. My most constant companion in childhood was my older brother Ralph. With rather less than two years separating us we were enough of an age to share experience, but far enough apart for our roles of his dominance and my submission to be firmly fixed. So much of our shared lives included nobody else, that we evolved quite an elaborate system of private communication. Of course we had our secret code of spoken words – what childhood friends don't? But we also had a code of whistles, piercing blasts on the brass cases of cartridges from Father's Winchester .44 carbine, that carried great distances even across the convoluted land over which we roamed. To locate, summon with varying degrees of urgency, warn of danger, check on health and safety, confirm or question messages – all these could be achieved with nothing more sophisticated than an inch and a half of brass tube. Yet even this was crude compared with the telepathic communication we achieved in our closest moments. Fear and distress especially were often communicated with complete disregard for physical distance.

We were so similar, yet so different. I responded to the emotionally sterile climate by creating a friendly, outgoing manner that attracted attention; his response was to become withdrawn, surly, and rebellious. I sought attention and approval; he shunned both. I bowed to authority and became part of the system; he fought it and remained an outsider. Whether it be explained in terms of karma or genetics, there is no doubt that from our earliest days we processed our experience with very different programmes.

So where was love? It was there behind all the hard, practical attitudes and behaviours of survival, but stowed very fully away. Never mentioned – never a kiss or a cuddle to make it live. Again memory plays me false. There was one spontaneous cuddle from my father as we sat together in the back seat of a car. I still feel the warmth of his old army greatcoat as I pretended to resist the unfamiliar contact. Perhaps my warmest adult contact was with Old Bill, the illiterate, toothless Irish ploughman who adopted me as toddler and took me with him whenever he was working near the homestead.

Was I happy? I remember many happy times. Not much detail, but times when life felt good and worth having. Like the day when self-consciousness struck. I was riding my bike to school, when I suddenly knew that I was a free being, with power of choice, in command of myself and the bike. I could decide whether to continue to school or turn back. I could make the bike turn left or right, stop or go faster, as I liked. To confirm my freedom I made the tyres trace figures-of-eight in the dust of the road, and even turned a few tight circles before deciding to carry on to school. Life would never be the same again. Of course I knew that Father's slightest wish, however subtly conveyed, was to be obeyed on pain of rejection, but somewhere behind that compulsion, from here on there was choice. If only in imagination, I could do what I decided to, and nobody else could take that power of choice from me.

A cameo from about that time. One tragic season I fell in love with a Southdown lamb which was proudly displayed at the school judging day, and even took prizes at the great Stratford A&P Show. Southdown lambs were bred not for five or six years of wool production, but for meat. My lamb wore the red ribbon of first in her class as she trotted after me in the grand parade at the end of the show. Waiting at the exit, the butcher who had bought her took off the ribbon, hung it round my neck, and carried the lamb away. Tears were not appropriate. For the long drive home I sat alone in the back seat of the car, numb and confused, the ribbon still round my neck. Did my parents deliberately let this drama play itself out to teach me the hard facts of farm life? Was this why they were so quiet on that long drive? Or did they just not understand that I loved that lamb, I wanted to hold her tight to my aching body, smell her warm, lanolin smell, cry rivers of tears into her tightly curled wool and tell her I never meant to let this happen. I never found out. We didn't talk about things like that. Since grief was obviously unacceptable, grief was very soon put firmly away. Life went on without it. Strangely, although with memory's eye I can see every detail of that little Southdown's shape, colour, and texture, hear her indignant voice demanding to be fed, even hear the simultaneous sneeze and fart with which she finished each bottle, her name is gone, I suspect for ever.

To some degree, all events of my childhood life, were coloured by my hated body. I was fat. I was big, podgy, clumsy, and slow. At least that's how I saw myself. There is some objective evidence to support that view – photographs, and a memory of trying to take pride in the fact that I weighed 130 pounds at the age of nine. That Ralph could outrun me and out-distance me in endurance I never attributed to his two years' seniority; it was the shameful burden of my fat body, which in my childhood mind was punishment for eating too much, for indulgence.

I accepted the great changes in my life at the age of ten with the resignation and lack of question long since learned from Father. Old Bill astonished the valley by taking the head shepherd's mother (after a proper church wedding), to share his retirement in New Plymouth, and Ralph went to boarding school. The immediate consequence of Ralph's disappearance was that I inherited Trixie.

Trixie was a petite black-and-tan bitch, mostly border collie in spite of her colour. A cocked ear and one upper lip permanently perched on top of the lower canine gave her a quizzical look. On the odd occasion when both upper lips were so lifted she wore a cheeky grin, which she often lived up to. Trained to nine command whistles, she never made a suggestion of a mistake while working, although she was not above questioning me if she thought I was giving silly orders. With Trixie as a partner I was suddenly raised from the status of junior rouseabout to part-time shepherd. And I had found a friend. Privately I began for the first time to question Father's wisdom. 'Take care not to become too fond of your dog. She's a worker, not a pet.' Surely Trixie was a worker, a working partner, and with far too much dignity to be called a mere pet, but she was a friend, whom I came to love dearly (and secretly).

It wasn't long before I confirmed the status of shepherd by acquiring two more dogs, one a cheerful, willing, and rather stupid English Sheepdog, and the other, one of Trixie's daughters, almost as endearing and accomplished as her mother. So I joined Father and the other shepherds on the musters, which sometimes meant riding out from home by 3 a.m. to be on my allotted beat by dawn. Perhaps I would be late for school, or not make it at all that day. But by this time the war had started. Now there was plenty of money – armies wear wool, or they did in 1940 – but so little labour that even a ten-year-old's contribution was needed.

So apart from the irksome business of having to go to school for most of the week, I now lived in the world of men, doing a man's job, and growing closer to Father. As well as many practical skills, he taught me self-reliance – there was nobody else to do it, so one worked out how to do it oneself. For his approval I took on responsibilities far beyond my years. Too proud to ask, I worked out how to make and hang gates, to mend harnesses, and a hundred other tasks that came my way. And I learned to shoot. Father was the local champion with all sorts of firearms. He was happy to teach me – I was a model pupil. He liked rabbit, stuffed with herbs and roasted – I shot rabbits with a .22 rifle. He disliked rats in the wool shed – I shot rats with an air rifle so as not to damage the corrugated iron walls. He complained of pheasants raiding the garden – I shot pheasants with a

12-bore gun whose noise and kick were frightening, but worth tolerating for the praise. Mother, too, found my skill useful. 'Before you go to school, would you go and shoot those magpies that are upsetting the hens?' So I shot magpies. Praise came, too, from the bushmen and the shepherds. A hand clapping me on the shoulder – not Father's hand, but at least the hand of a grown man who knew of these things – as a magpie fell from a high tree. 'You're an artist, Robin – an artist!'

And there was money to earn. Possum skins were now a good price – they were needed for fighter pilots' gloves, or so I was told. How did a ten-year-old bring himself to use that abomination, the gin trap? But I did just that. A possum caught by one leg clamped in steel jaws, there to wait until I came in the morning to release it from its agony by beating it on the head with an iron bar. This was commendable enterprise, approved by Father and his world. This was evil karma, serving to bury deep and ever deeper not only my childish aspiration to compassion, but my very ability to experience and respond to love. These faculties were to lie largely suppressed for forty-five years, until meditation and the response to a loving friend could begin their work of restoration.

# 8

# boarding school

There was never any question about my going to Nelson College. Ralph was already there, only a year ahead of me. There was no reason to go anywhere else. Yet, at the age of twelve, the thought of travelling away from home, a whole day on the train, then a night on the Cook Strait Ferry, was horrifying. Twelve weeks – three months – of being separated from home by an infinity of land was barely tolerable. Being banished beyond the blue salt ocean was unthinkable. Yet it was inevitable. Boys, especially bright ones, went to secondary school. If they lived in Mangamingi, they went to boarding school. Part of me cursed the fates that made me different from Buster or Herbie, farm boys who would always be farm boys, whose education beyond the limits of the Mangamingi school would be in the hands of farmer-fathers. They didn't have to go away to Nelson for three months. Yet part of me knew already that there was more to life than back country sheep farming, and that finding it meant boarding school. And I was my father's son, well trained in acceptance of fate with resignation and lack of complaint.

Could the experience of boarding school have been as miserable as my memories tell me? Reflection tells me not, but I am inclined to let uncensored imagination have its say before investigating too far. It is these memories, after all, that have coloured my subsequent life. Things would surely have been worse had it not been for Ralph's advice, delivered in one of my moments of darkest misery, miraculously finding the way open to the depth of my aching heart. 'It's up to you how miserable you feel. If you try all the time to think of the bits that aren't so bad, you won't spend so much time in the really bad bits.' Time and time again those words lifted me from paralysing despair, helping me to shoulder my burdens and trudge on.

The dormitories were designed to house eight beds each, but they were crammed with ten or twelve. Night after night a boy lies huddled under the blankets, face buried in pillow to drown his sobs, body held rigid to prevent the straw mattress from advertising his convulsions of misery. Much of the day had been given to longing for the privacy of the darkened bed, to allow tears to flow without heaping ridicule on already intolerable grief.

The shock of discovering the officially-condoned bullying of the fagging system. I found myself taken over by Red Sinclair, a notorious loud-mouthed bully, from whom, after an initial terrifying show of strength, I received totally unexpected kindness. In fact the coarse speech and rough manner hid a shy country boy, who quickly recognized one of his kind. I suspect that his selecting me from the line-up of available new boys arose from a precursor of this recognition. It was Red who advised me how to keep my head down, how to sidestep trouble, and, when the going got rough, how to escape to the Memorial Reference Library. This was a place of silence, hallowed by even the grossest of bullies, in which I frequently took refuge, pretending to study whatever book fell to hand while waiting for my tormentors to go away.

Compulsory sports, especially rugby and gymnastics. My clumsy fat body was quite incapable of the things demanded of it, which was a source of untold merriment to instructors and spectators alike. From these ordeals there was no escape.

How did I meet these shocks to my established world? What I did as well or better than most was generally not given high value by my peers. Being near the top of the class in most academic subjects did much to help my relationship with teachers, but nothing at all to endear me to my fellow pupils. In sports I could swim passably well, especially when I was able to put my greater buoyancy to advantage for long distance work. Perhaps it was because of the war that rifle shooting was held in high esteem. For whatever reason, my skill with a rifle soon became a major route to acceptance by my peers. The only boy in the school who usually beat me in rifle competitions was Ralph, which did nothing to detract from its acceptance value for me. In fact I was able to cash in on his glory as one of the boys from the backwoods who must have been born with a rifle in their hands.

But my overall response to a system I could neither beat nor ignore was to join it. As I became more senior in the school hierarchy, I became more integrated with the system, until by my final year I must have been nothing short of an impossible prig. I find myself wincing in shame as I recall the degree to which I identified with the system of authority. In the School Cadets I was sergeant of the prize-winning platoon. As a prefect I upheld authority to the letter. Like Lewis Carroll's oysters, my hair was brushed, my face was washed, my shoes were clean and neat. My behaviour, at least in public, was exemplary. (Out of the public eye there were a few peccadillos, such as enjoying an innocent cuddle with the housemaster's daughter in his living room when the family was out. If this were known it could not have avoided severe censure – it behoves a pretty, seventeen-year-old girl surrounded by large numbers of lonely boys to be a model of propriety.) However, the demands boarding school made on me required major adaptive changes. In response, I at least survived the five years of incarceration with minimal damage to myself or anybody else. In retrospect, it could have been much worse.

This is not intended to be another *Tom Brown's Schooldays*. It is an attempt to recall events, thoughts, and emotions from a period of my life of which I have great difficulty remembering anything. It was an unhappy time. The memory of my response to it brings me no satisfaction. This exercise, then, seeks lessons that may have been buried under that aversion; guides to my teenage development that may point to further remedial action to be taken now. Perhaps pointers to later problems, especially to the development of alcohol addiction, the symptoms of which began not many years after I left school.

Of course, the experience has left its scars. Just forty-seven years after I left boarding school I had a series of nightmares relating to those unhappy years. I could find nothing in my present circumstances to account for the dreams, until I realized that at the Buddhist convention I was about to attend I would meet two or three hundred people, most of whom I didn't know, I would be attending lectures, eating in a large communal dining room, and sleeping in a dormitory. With the exception of the large numbers, this had all been familiar experience in recent years. What was different was that because it was to be such a large gathering, a boarding school had been hired for the purpose.

With hindsight it is obvious that my emotional security was so tenuous at the age of twelve that it just would not stand separation from my sources of support. Yet how could it have been managed better? I have no doubt that my parents did the best they could with what their stunted emotional development had given them. I never asked either of them whether they knew how unhappy I was, and if so, how they managed that knowledge. It is unlikely that I would have adapted better had I been sent to one of the two possible secondary schools nearer home, with a view to coming home for the occasional weekend. In fact, the decision to send me far away was made in the belief that I would settle down better because home visits would be out of the question.

There were of course the holidays. However painful the time at school, it occupied only forty weeks of the year. For the other twelve I was rouseabout, junior shepherd, pack team leader, truck driver, or whatever other farm function had to be fulfilled. It never occurred to me, or to anybody else concerned, that during the school holidays there could be any occupation other than on the farm. Besides which, the war continued until almost the end of my schooldays. Everybody worked for the war effort. In my society everybody worked anyway. That's what distinguished responsible people from layabouts, shirkers, and other riff-raff.

My memory is that those short periods spent as part of the farm workforce were happy times. One or two of 'my' dogs remained faithful to me, or at least could be persuaded, if their present owners were not about, to travel with me and work for me. Working for Father as part of the team gave me a sense of identity and purpose. There was exercise too for my special skill with firearms. The meagre ration of ammunition issued for the control of pests was passed mainly to me because I could use it effectively. Wild pigs had become something of a menace while there had been nobody hunting them. So a rifle or home-made pistol was part of the harness as I rode the hills for whatever purpose. There was always the fear that a sheepdog, its hunting instinct roused by a chance encounter with a boar, would be injured in the skirmish, unless the pig could be killed swiftly. Feral goats, too, had overrun the wilder parts of the hills. Many bloody days were given to their destruction.

From so many years away, seen against the grim life of boarding school, those periods of farm life could so easily be romanticized. It was not always easy. In fact disillusion came – if ever illusion there were – in the spring of 1946. Three thousand ewes were lambing, as they had lambed for many years, over large tracts of rugged hills. I vividly remember twenty-six consecutive days of riding the hills, seeking out and attending to the lambing. The weather was appalling, howling southerly winds and rain, three worn-out horses, one day scrambling over slippery hill tracks and two days recovering, dogs too tired to leave their kennels in the morning, a gale blowing up a steep hillside catching under my oilskin coat and threatening to hurl me from my horse into the Patea River hundreds of feet below. The indelible vision of my hat spiralling down into the river an impossible distance below still stirs a trace of nausea and a prickling in the back of the neck. How much historical fact is contained in these memories is open to question, but what is beyond doubt is that I decided at that point of my life that sheep farming was not for me. I would wear dry clothes, go to university, and become a country vet, or possibly a family doctor.

# 9

# university

I was 17 when I approached Victoria College (now Victoria University) in Wellington, a man of the world, capable, confident, and (with the escalating demand for wool) relatively affluent. I was also timid, emotionally stunted, and fearfully ignorant of life. I found myself at home in the company of men five to ten years older than myself, men who had experienced the extended adolescence of army or air force life, even the horrors of war. Together we studied basic sciences, sorted out the iniquities of the world, and hid our emotional immaturity with quantities of alcohol. Within its limitations, this way of life met my needs. In spite of the age difference I found myself deferred to, both in my ability to think and argue and in the resistance to alcohol that was to contribute in future years to the addiction that threatened my life. In fact, in many ways I was the leader of the group.

In the course of my first year at Victoria I also had an experience that pointed the way to my future spiritual path. The exercise one day was to search a drop of pond water for microscopic life. Here was a world that for me was new, exciting, and before this moment quite unsuspected, a world of minute life forms, all motionless or near it – except for one. This was paramecium, a slipper-shaped, single-celled animal swimming so vigorously around its hanging drop that I had difficulty keeping track of it. Like the light of a new day the realization struck me: here was a free-living animal, one of uncountable millions of free-living animals populating the world, all in some mysterious way interconnected. From paramecium through myself to the blue whale, all of life was one great web of interdependent beings. Through half a lifetime this little insight was to expand through animism and pantheism to a strong and sustaining religious belief that I was to discover – thirty-five years later – was Buddhism.

The world was struggling to restore a semblance of stability from the post-war chaos. Universities were stretching themselves to the limit to absorb the deluge of returning ex-combatants seeking education and vocational training. Of the 110 places in its second-year class for 1948 the Otago Medical School was able to accommodate only seven non-priority students from Victoria. My ranking from the hundred-odd applicants was eighth. For a few minutes I was devastated – I was not accustomed to failure – until it occurred to me that remaining at Victoria to complete a science degree as a entry ticket to Medical School was not an unattractive prospect.

By the end of my second year in Wellington, perspectives on life had changed completely. I now owned a nearly-new Morris Minor, I was established in a residential college, and was overwhelmingly, devastatingly in love. In common with all my friends, Christine was some years older than I was, a shy, gentle young woman with a flattering appreciation of my practical skills and much more experience of the world than I had. As the time approached for me to work on the farm over the summer, she casually slipped into the conversation the unthinkable suggestion that there could be other places to work; Wellington, for instance. She was clever enough not to hint that I might not work at all. That would have caused me to question her grip on reality. So I became a temporary union member in my first and only forty-hour-a-week job, as a porter at the Wellington Public Hospital.

A few hours of undemanding work each day, a pay packet each Thursday, and every evening free to spend with Christine. This was as near to heaven as I could imagine. How grateful I was for the Returned Services Priority which had for the second year put me at the head of the Medical School's 'sorry, no place for you this year' list. I was in absolutely no hurry to move to a strange town in the wintry south to begin the rigorous life of a medical student. Then the axe fell. On the first day of the new academic year a telegram from Dunedin, 'A cancellation for the 1949 Second Year Class at the Otago Medical School has made a place available for you. Please notify your acceptance immediately and enrol as soon as possible.' An evening of tearful farewell (tearful on Christine's part – it would be many years before I learned to weep), a day cancelling arrangements for the year in Wellington and packing my possessions into the Morris Minor, a night ferry to Christchurch, and a long, lonely drive through tumultuous emotions to a new life. That I might delay a year to enjoy more of the delights of Wellington never occurred to me.

The Medical School was a subculture within the subculture of the University within the subculture of the relatively isolated southern city of Dunedin. Sharing the overwhelming intensity of lectures, laboratories, and study, as well as the first shock of the dissecting room in whose carbolic atmosphere we spent four full afternoons each week for two years, catalysed the development of friendships.

Student parties, of course, happened spontaneously, whenever the pressure of life demanded release. Although alcohol was an essential part of all such gatherings, just as important were items supplied by all and sundry. Television had not yet invaded our lives, nor had cheap pop records. If we wanted entertainment we did it ourselves. I soon found that I had some skill as a raconteur and ballad singer, later as a member of a barber-shop quartet, which gave me entry to student flats all over town. All this nurtured the alcohol dependence that was progressively to overshadow my life. How fortunate I was that more dangerous drugs had not yet become popular.

Through two laborious years of pre-clinical studies to Medicine, Surgery, Pathology, Obstetrics, Psychiatry. This was all about real people, sick people, people I could help to be well. This was what I had come so far to find. But was it really? During these years a faint discomfort grew into a howling protest. This was all about diseases, treatments, cures, not about real people at all. Indeed, lip service was paid to human beings, to people with feelings, with children, parents or lovers, with happiness and pain, but if I were to believe the teaching, my work was with diseases, with manipulation of physiology, biochemistry, and anatomy. What was health? In spite of protestations to the contrary, health was absence of demonstrable, diagnosable, treatable disease. And where was death? Death was failure, by implication even culpable failure, to be studied for whatever lessons it may offer then put aside lest it divert energy from important things. Death was not to be acknowledged as a natural part of the process of life. I remember no training in helping people to die – much less in helping relatives and friends to adjust their own lives to it. Death was a process to be managed by others, not by physicians or surgeons trained in scientific medicine. Of course I exaggerate. There was a great deal of good teaching, some excellent teaching from outstanding clinicians, but through all of it shone the hard light of science relegating kindness and compassion to a Cinderella role. For a few years, natural empathy for my fellow beings retreated, bowing to superior wisdom, but fortunately for me and my patients it eventually reasserted itself to take over its true role.

My final year took me back to Wellington Hospital, this time in student's white jacket with tools of the trade ostentatiously projecting from pockets. It was a good year. Contact with sick people was closer;

I was even able to take a little responsibility for management of cases. As the end of the year approached, I applied, along with most of the class, for a post as House Surgeon at the Wellington Public Hospital for the following year, and was not accepted. Suddenly the world was challenging me to make decisions for myself. Who did I know to appeal to? Arthur, two years my senior and one-time member of the party quartet, was surgical registrar at New Plymouth. A phone call,

'Arthur, what can I do about getting a job?'

'We're short of a man here.'

'Sounds good, can you send me the application form?'

'Don't need one. Job's yours!'

So was arranged my first professional post. No formal interview with my prospective chiefs, and to the best of my memory, nothing discussed, written, or contracted.

# 10

# career

November 1953 saw both my twenty-fourth birthday and my graduation MBChB (Otago). Most of my time over the few years since I had moved south, I had been doing what I did best, academic study, so the days had passed happily enough. But I had not done much growing as an individual – nor, for that matter, did anybody else in that mad scramble for qualifications and the licence to practise. So although I was skilled in many things by the time I graduated, and in many ways much older than my years, emotionally I had little matured since leaving Wellington.

Stacking my possessions – including the precious Bachelor of Medicine and Bachelor of Surgery diplomas – in the Morris Minor, I wended my way to New Plymouth to become a resident house surgeon, one of a team of six, of whom two others were as newly minted as I. On Christmas Eve, four weeks after I began working as clerk and surgical assistant to one of the general surgeons, Mount Ruapehu erupted, sending a lahar down the Whangaehu River to sweep away the Tangiwai bridge under the wheels of a crowded train. Like iron filings to a magnet, surgeons from over 100 miles away were drawn to the scene of the disaster. Left behind to manage as best we could was the team of juniors, pooling our minimal experience to handle whatever emergencies arose.

I had reason to thank Father for his early teaching. If there's nobody else to do it, do it yourself, as best you can. Learn from mistakes, but don't let them distract you from the next decision. As I look back on those few days I am appalled at the responsibilities we had to take on. When the senior staff returned and reassembled their teams, we paused to take stock. We had all learned to swim, with no calamities.

So as experience accumulated, art and techniques were absorbed from teachers and from daily contact with injury and disease. Precarious dependence on approval drove me to become an expert and sought-after assistant. It was in the operating theatre that the practical resourcefulness learned at my father's knee was especially appreciated, so I almost became a surgeon.

Many of the major decisions in life just happened, perhaps to be rationalized later. That was how I came to be in London for most of my postgraduate training. It was all because of the New Plymouth Hospital Ball. Arthur, the surgical registrar who was my immediate senior, asked me to partner his sister, a professional pianist home from London on a brief visit. I never fully understood Doris's interest, but for me it was fascination from the start. I had never met anybody so sophisticated, so dynamic, so au fait with the cultural life of the big city. Maybe we just fell in love. For whatever reason, I accepted not only her suggestion that London was where the widest medical experience was to be gained, but also an oblique hint that becoming a Freemason would be just the thing to get me into the right places. Perhaps her father being a senior officer in the local lodge had something to do with both the decision and my rapid transit through the junior grades of Freemasonry. Be that as it may, a few brief months later, when I signed on as surgeon on the *Port Wellington*, a passenger-carrying freighter bound for London, a Master Mason's apron was carefully stowed in my suitcase.

These days it is hard to imagine how the journey was accomplished only half a century ago. Two fleets of refrigerated freighters maintained a regular delivery of frozen meat from here to there, and manufactured goods from there to here. Many carried twelve first-class passengers – which necessitated carrying a doctor. The pay was threepence a week, plus a first-class passage, for about an hour's work each day.

London. One could have been excused for thinking Victoria Dock an unromantic entrance to the hub of the world, but it was not so for me on that cold, drizzly April evening. The tugs nudged the ship into its berth against a quay deserted but for two dock workers handling the ungainly hawsers, and a solitary woman leaning against the wall of a dingy warehouse. I scarcely looked at her until a voice from the bridge broke through my fantasies of the great city. 'Is that a friend of yours?' somehow Doris had not only discovered where and when we were to berth but had found her way past the guarded gates to be there to greet me. Oblivious to the protocols of shore-going in a foreign port, I stepped ashore to greet my long lost lover appropriately, and disappear with her into the depths of the sprawling city that was to be my home for the next four years. There were no comments when

I returned to the ship at dawn, or when I formally signed off from the ship's company later in the day. It was some months before I discovered that the ship's officers had gone to some lengths to prevent the authorities intercepting me.

The rounds of sight-seeing and concert-going (as an insider, Doris had access to the best seats) could not go on for ever. I was still far from outgrowing the work ethic learned at my father's knee. The fact that I was in London to be with Doris was carefully concealed under the acceptable purpose of postgraduate education. That meant joining the army of recently-qualified colonials seeking to apprentice themselves to the big-name teachers at the London hospitals. The art, I very soon discovered, was to track down these doyens not in their famous teaching hospitals – those positions were always filled by their own graduates – but in the peripheral hospitals which they condescended to visit in their chauffeur-driven Rolls-Royces. After the new and sobering experience of attending several interviews only to see some scruffy Australian or South African appointed ahead of me, I eventually secured a job at Barnet General Hospital, where I was shared by a famous dermatologist and soon-to-be-famous physician from St Bartholomew's. Most of my day there was spent in an ancient brick building whose stone steps were worn into deep hollows, and said to have been Oliver Twist's workhouse. Compared with New Plymouth it was a breeze. Luxurious quarters complete with bar, billiard room, and tennis courts, shared with about a dozen others, and no more than two or three nights a week on call. And it was only twenty minutes in my new Standard Ten from Doris's flat on the edge of Hampstead Heath. But, as I was to learn from Buddhist teachings many years later, all things are impermanent.

It soon became obvious that Doris's plan was to become a concert pianist based in London, with me as the socially and financially supportive husband. Mine was to become a suburban family doctor in New Zealand, with Doris as the supportive wife. Some aspects of these plans were apparently incompatible. Doris departed for Paris to take up a long-term scholarship while I, increasingly lonely and isolated by more and more demanding appointments at a variety of hospitals, pursued my own education. So it was that when I met Ysabel, whom I had known in Wellington, now also lonely in the big city, we fell into each other's arms and, as was the custom in those days, married 'until death do us part'. We didn't survive quite as long as that, but it was thirty years and five children later that our ways finally parted.

Like many of my decisions to date, getting married happened rather than being chosen. So, too, did Ysabel's immediate pregnancy. A decision that could have led me to the striped trousers and Rolls-Royce of Harley Street was narrowly averted. For something over a year I worked as a resident at the prestigious Royal Masonic Hospital in Hammersmith. My chiefs were senior Freemasons, authors of accepted textbooks in their fields and mostly connected with the Royal Household. It was all very seductive to a lad from the colonies. Following one or more of these august presences into their private practices was both possible and, for a while, tempting. Fortunately, before taking any irrevocable steps, I came to my senses. Returning to my original plan of becoming a family doctor in New Zealand was one of the few really conscious decisions that I took while I was in London. Having made that decision, I again allowed myself to be carried by the tide of circumstance. Various events took me to Auckland's North Shore to help a friend of a friend whose general practice was overloaded, for 'about six weeks', but those six weeks soon grew into a partnership that was to last for over thirty years.

The degree to which I allowed major decisions to make themselves was not a good preparation, one might think, for a lifetime of making decisions of great importance to others. But how many of the decisions that shape our lives result from mature consideration? How much more often do they emerge from a tangle of likes and dislikes, largely unconscious, to be later graced by reasons dreamed up by an inventive intellect? Decisions made on behalf of others, although still influenced by our unconscious views, attitudes, and desires, are likely to have a larger content of true judgement. So neither should I be too hard on my younger self, nor should I wonder too much at my temerity in accepting responsibility for so much of other people's lives. Many years after the events that took me into family medicine, I met a phrase in the writing of Sangharakshita, the founder of the Western Buddhist Order, that described me so well: 'A bundle of conflicting desires and selves loosely tied together with a name and address.' Which of us who is not consciously following a spiritual path can claim to have moved far beyond this state?

# 11

# becoming a family doctor

Seeking the nature of positive health seemed a lonely quest, although I'm sure there were many others on the same path as lonely as I. There was little enough guidance in my undergraduate teaching.

The prevailing attitudes of medical school I remember very well. We had talked a lot about sickness and recovery, about pathology and correction of pathology. The talk about good health, well-being, and recovery from illness or operations was free and glib. But the real study and effort was to do with sickness. It was disease and pathology that occupied my mind, and became the angle from which I saw life.

There was an imposing red textbook on gynaecology, whose introduction went deep into the thesis that gynaecology was the study of Woman from all aspects, not just her reproductive function, and especially not just her reproductive pathology. Two pages further on came the chapter headings 'Diseases of the Nipple', 'Diseases of the Breast', 'Diseases of the Vulva', 'Diseases of....' Not one word, not a thought, about healthy, happy Woman, about her living and loving, about her society and her cosmos. All this was severe conditioning. To my credit, I did fight this tendency as best I could. But even deeper was the conditioning towards approval. I was limited in how much I could question, show disagreement, challenge, for fear of rejection or ridicule. So I gave lip-service to healthy, happy, heroic Woman, and devoted my mind to diseases of the vulva.

When in due course Woman appeared seeking help in my consulting room, I found myself meeting her as a nipple, breast, vulva, vagina, etc. She was all of these, with their diseases congenital, neoplastic, inflammatory, degenerative, metabolic, traumatic, and functional. As she opened her mouth to communicate, what I heard was less the joy and sorrow of her living than a veiled, symbolic descriptions of her parts and their dysfunctions. And that was only the beginning. Old people tended to be Geriatrics, Diseases of Old Age, Pathology of Degeneration. Old people may well have been telling me of the wisdom of experience, of the joy of fulfilled relationships, but what I heard was Degenerative Disease. It did not stop there. The Woman and the Old Person, the Child and the Worker, all became conditioned by the same enveloping malady. So often I was told, 'I don't know why I am here, doctor. I am not sick really. There is nothing wrong with me. I just don't feel well.'

I have no memory of pausing at the outset of my career as a family doctor to ask myself some very basic questions. What were health and disease? What was my role in health and disease? What were my expectations of myself? What were the expectations of those who were to employ me? How well did my training at medical school and the subsequent series of hospitals prepare me for what lay ahead? Who were the people I was to work with? Who was I? What was the purpose of our lives? It seems unbelievable that I could have launched myself into working, day and night, among the sick and suffering without having asked these questions.

Meeting living people while alone and unsupported was a serious shock. Until this point in my life I had been a member of a team, always with a senior colleague to call on if things got beyond me. Now I met my patients face to face with nothing to hide behind, protected only by my growing confidence and increasing awareness of a natural empathy with my fellow human beings. The lessons came thick and fast.

Sean, an Apollo-like figure in his middle thirties, strode into the consulting room like an advertisement for a health farm.

'Need a check-up, Doc.'

We went through the usual questions and physical examination without turning up any sign of pathology, but behind the façade of robust health was a man in pain.

'Sean, why did you come to see me?'

'I need your help, Doc. As you say, I'm as fit as a flea. I've got a wonderful wife and two lovely boys. I've reached the top of the ladder at work. I have a beautiful house with the best view on the coast, and I drive a Mark IX Jag. Everything I've ever wanted. What do I do now?'

With increasing frequency I found myself commenting to patients that I couldn't find anything wrong with their state of health, but that there was a limit to how positively healthy they could be unless they had a good idea of who they were and where they fitted into the universe.

I can't remember the legitimate, 'I came here for a medical check, not a sermon,' objection ever being voiced. However, I did on several occasions find myself in even deeper water.

'You could be right. Where do I go for help with that one?' This was beyond my brief and training. 'Umm, do you know anybody who is involved with a church?'

'I play golf with a priest, but I wouldn't talk to him about it. Besides which, I was brought up in his church and I chucked it in. A lot of nonsense!'

The question Sean raised, as did so many others over the years, was not one that a thirty-year-old, just-out-of-school family doctor could meet with a quick answer. Sean had no sign of disease, nor even depression in the medical sense. He was a man without a purpose, or rather a man whose conscious purpose was set too low to meet his needs. Obviously, he needed a higher target, a vision that would necessitate lifting himself above his present mundane values, a challenge worthy of his mettle. How was he to find it? Who could guide him towards it? Who could guide me towards a more inspiring sense of purpose than that of meeting the immediate problem in my consulting room and providing financial security for my family?

Time and again arose the question: how well have we been served by the split between physician and priest? Where is the dividing line between hygiene and ethics? For a long time I put these questions in the 'too hard' basket, promising myself that I would think them through one day.

In the course of time, I began to realize that if there were a state of being unwell, and since so many people suffered from it, there must be a state of being well. Somebody, somewhere, must have thought this one through and described the state of being well. Perhaps the World Health Organization? But their definition, dredged up from long-buried memory, described only a state of 'physical, emotional, and social well-being', and that was not very warm or satisfying.

For some time I sought wellness by looking at disease in the hope of seeing the other pole of the duality. Then it occurred to me that if I found people who were superlatively well, I could see what it was they had in abundance. Perhaps athletes whose bodies were in such superb shape? Ken was one such. For a while I put him on a pedestal labelled 'health', until he came to me complaining that his drinking was interfering with his training, that both were interfering with his marriage, and was there any help for him? Down tumbled Ken from his pedestal. Jane, the happy young mother I often saw at the kindergarten? Such lovely children, such a serene smile. And, as I found out not much later, such a pig of a husband, such poverty and privation.

I soon found that nobody was really healthy, even in the WHO sense. This began to trouble me deeply. Was I really working only to remove obvious pathology, or was there an ideal state towards which I could guide people – including myself? A common yardstick was the ability to carry out one's normal duties, care for children, to earn one's living at a socially acceptable job, and so on. But there had to be more to health than that. And why be healthy, whatever that was, if you weren't happy? Just to get rid of an immediate pain did no more than that; it didn't get you any nearer to happiness. It meant no more than the satisfaction of an immediate need. In no time, another took its place. Slowly it dawned on me that this was just about trying to remove obvious negatives. Pains, dysfunctions of all sorts, might be removed, and the result would be health? Obviously not. Where was the positive thing I could call health? It had to have something to do with happiness. That was as far as my understanding of positive health advanced until much later in my career.

Years later – many years later – it occurred to me that the meeting point of priest and physician was in happiness. Although neither talks much about happiness, both are intimately concerned with it. So what is happiness? Here began a train of thought that I wished I had set in motion long ago.

Happiness is hard to define, but it must have something to do with emotional positivity. My first thought is that it arises from an ongoing sense of purpose. Can I be happy if I don't have a conscious purpose, an ideal, a vision towards which I direct my life? If I can't – and it certainly seems that I can't – then why not? How does a purpose become a vision? What tells me whether a purpose is 'good' or 'bad'? Somehow a good purpose must be associated with universally accepted good motives, those motives that many years later I was to hear Buddhists refer to as skilful: generosity, love, and a yearning for understanding. If I define my purpose, what else do I need? I need love and longing for that purpose, sufficient to power the determination to work towards it. I need to be confident that I can attain it, or at least approach it, and I need to be actually trying to do that. I need to be free from obvious barriers to these things, like a mixed-up mind or

grossly impaired senses. I need to be free from beliefs that will prevent me making progress. And I need energy to apply to the task. All
this could be called faith, if that word hadn't acquired so many confusing associations. And together with this I need what is commonly
known as good health.

Is happiness, then, the product of good health and a sense of
ongoing purpose? Let me assume that it is, and see if I can find
anything missing. Suppose I have discovered my ideal and have confidence in it. I know from the example of others and my own experience that I can move towards it. My mind functions well and is
reasonably clear. I am not stuck with totally inhibiting views of the
nature of myself and the universe. I have an active urge to move
towards a conscious ideal, and the emotional energy to power it. And
I have a reasonably sound body through which to interact with the
world. In fact even this last is not totally necessary; I have seen a wonderful sense of happiness in people whom I would have thought
severely deprived. Helen comes to mind. Old – she must have been
over 80 when I last saw her – blind, or so near it it didn't matter, and
with such grossly damaged lungs that her every breath was a labour. I
think she would have been happier in a better body, but even that is
uncertain. Helen spent her life meditating on all aspects of existence,
and was among the most loved – and happiest – people I have met. I
used to take my students to see how completely it was possible to live,
in spite of (or perhaps because of) her appalling handicaps. However,
for most of us, reasonably good health seems to be one of the pre-
requisites for happiness.

One final requirement, over which neither physician nor priest
has much control, is the absence of overwhelming external burdens
such as poverty, oppression, and natural disaster.

If I could use the term 'health' to denote the positive state I
have just described, the equation becomes, 'health is the product of
good health in the medical sense, plus an ongoing sense of purpose,
or – if you can accept the term – faith,' which must be as cogent an
argument for the re-establishment of the role of physician-priest as we
could find.

An afterthought. How much justification is there, then, for a life
devoted to the promotion of health alone? In its limited way it is very
useful, and becomes much more so if it is practised with awareness of
the wider aspects of health, even if this seems to be outside the doctor's brief. That is pretty well what my life as family doctor was given

over to, even if for the most part 'faith' was rudimentary. I believe that for all of my working life I was conscious that awareness of purpose was the basis for positive health. It took a long time for that awareness to mature.

# 12

# the family doctor

There was one small problem about moving into family medicine that I had never noticed because it didn't occur to me that things could be different: there was absolutely no vocational training available. I had acquired a great deal of knowledge about the function of the human body in health and sickness, some about the human mind, and a little about the emotions. Many were the focal points of knowledge; few the threads that wove them into wisdom. I can hardly blame myself for this state of affairs. Training programmes in family medicine did not exist. The process of integration of knowledge into understanding happened – if at all – under the guidance of a senior colleague, if one were fortunate enough to have one nearby, or by trial and error. I say 'if at all' because this aspect of training was available only to the receptive. Since most learning up to this point of a medical career is concerned with hard facts and scientific truths, any receptivity to nuances of expression, veiled fear and guilt, or barely conscious messages flitting between family members at a bedside or in the consulting room, had no fertile ground in which to develop.

Several things favoured my learning. The first was moving into practice first as an assistant, then as a partner, to Ray, who had been finding his own way into the mysteries of family medicine for four years before I joined him. The second was that, starting my practice mostly among young families in a rapidly growing suburb, I was in the same situation myself. Much of my understanding of the joys and sorrows of young adults with small children came from personal experience. Perhaps most important was the fact that I was interested in people. I had never been taken over by the fascination with disease that governed many of my contemporaries.

One of the earliest tapestries of understanding woven from the unconnected threads of knowledge in my work-basket was to do with causation. In narrow, specialized fields, the factors leading to the present state of health or disease could usually be traced simply and directly to a small paragraph headed 'aetiology'. In daily life it was seldom so simple.

The so-called allergic disorders of children were among my earliest teachers, both because they were so common, and because my own children were afflicted by them. The stuffy, runny nose, with its complications of acute middle ear infection and the chronic glue ear that impaired hearing to produce speech and educational difficulties. The frank asthma, or the much more common recurrent cough, so often misdiagnosed as infection and treated – at great expense and often entailing further allergic problems for the child – with repeated courses of antibiotics. The great variety of itchy rashes, one of which I confidently diagnosed early in my career as a food allergy, only to have many of the child's classmates at an expensive school develop chickenpox two weeks later.

Sometimes the main cause was obvious. The child had itchy eyes and sneezes after cuddling her guinea pig, or developed itchy spots the day after the first strawberries of the season. More frequently it was not. One of my daughters developed asthma in October if she had school examinations coming up, if the wind was from the west, and there had been no rain for a few days. Seasonal dusts reached their critical concentrations only under specific climatic conditions, and then produced symptoms only in a child sensitized by a certain type of anxiety. She discovered for herself that closing her bedroom window overnight usually prevented the symptom.

I soon discovered that most problems in the department labelled 'children who sneeze, wheeze, and scratch' required full cooperation from the patient and parents, which in turn called for an effective method of explaining the situation to all. The child concerned – and often the whole family – was often called upon to make quite important changes in their habits, which – as I amply confirmed many years later when I entered the spiritual life – is not easy. A child with chronic hay fever, for instance, could be asked, hopefully with help from the rest of the family, to remove from the bedroom everything moveable, to vacuum clean, damp dust, or wash (where relevant) every surface and fabric of the room and such of the contents as were to be retrieved, and to return to the room only what was absolutely necessary. Thereafter, a regime of regular dust control was to continue indefinitely. Like so many of the changes we face in life, action had to be motivated by faith, since rewards could not be gained without investing a great deal of effort.

The concept of multiple causation was not easily grasped, sometimes even by physicians and family doctors. Yet somehow a mere child, and parents who might be uneducated and/or unintelligent, had to be led to enough understanding to motivate them to change. For this situation I evolved the game of 'don't let the dog jump over the wall,' the dog being the symptom, and the wall the child's defences against it. 'Somewhere along this wall,' I would explain to the child, 'is a heap of stones. If it gets high enough the dog can climb up and jump over, which causes your sneezes and headaches and sore ears. Now let's see if we can find what the biggest stones are, and try to take them away.' So the search would begin. 'It's worst when I wake up. And at Grandma's place. Grandma has a cat. The last time I stayed at her place the cat slept on my bed and it was terrible.' It often took imaginative analysis of a diary, maintained patiently for days or even months, before the more obscure, and often more important, factors revealed themselves. And so we named the stones in the pile, through dusts perennial and seasonal, foods, animals, people, emotional disturbances, and whatever else child, siblings, or parents could think of. Then came the problem of how to remove some, or perhaps only one, of the biggest stones and, hey presto, the dog couldn't get over the wall. Of course it wasn't always successful, but it was fun, and it usually developed a good working relationship between doctor and patient.

In my later years, when my chief interest moved from medicine to Buddhism, I came across the teaching of dependent origination, the foundation of all Buddhist philosophy. Essentially, it states that any phenomenon, be it an object or event, arises from the coming together of a multitude of causes, and itself becomes a cause for more phenomena. Change any of these causes and the phenomenon changes. How often in pondering the implications of this teaching have I thought of that game I played all those years ago with children who sneezed, wheezed, or scratched.

A person or a problem? All my medical teaching insisted that the patient was a whole person in an environment, not just a presenting symptom of a disease. But all my medical teachers were people who had emerged from their own conditioning, and therefore presented the truth from their own point of view. All of them had had scientific training, which had led them to a greater or lesser degree to believe that they saw reality objectively, that they were observers and interpreters of fact, that their own self view was not relevant to their understanding. I should therefore not have been too hard on myself when I realized just how much I subscribed to those same 'scientific' views when I first came to family medicine. It would have been possible to retain that attitude over the years. Many do, but only at the cost of refusing to see or empathize with the people who come for help.

It soon became evident that people not only had symptoms; they reacted to them. And the reaction often caused more distress than the original symptom. So the more threatening the possible consequences of the symptom to that particular person, the greater the element of reaction in their distress. It did not take me long to discover, for instance, that chest pain to many people signalled 'heart attack' and fear of death. If I could, with suitable evidence and confidence, pronounce that the pain was benign, the patient would usually depart happily, still with with their pain, now no longer a concern.

This lesson was driven home by an experience of becoming a patient myself. Being aware of noises in my head, I began to fear hearing loss that would impair my skill in detecting and interpreting those fascinating sounds which told the adept so much about the behaviour of heart and lungs. I had studied under physicians who had developed the art of the stethoscope to its ultimate. Electronic sound analysis had done much to unravel the secrets of the esoteric language of heart and lung, but had not invaded the consulting room far enough to displace the stethoscope as its chief transmitter. So hearing loss, especially high tone hearing loss, would have been a major disaster. Accordingly I consulted Jack, a local ENT specialist. I can hardly blame him for not understanding that my concern was with the detection of the ghostly voice of a leaking aortic valve, or the elusive, metallic quality of inspiration heard through a film of fluid covering the lung, rather than with a distant scream in my ears. I was only vaguely aware of it myself, until I heard, 'Hearing's normal. Can't do anything about the noises. Take these to help you tune into a different wavelength.' I didn't care about the noises, and I certainly didn't want to take a tranquillizer. I just wanted to be reassured about my hearing. But I hadn't told Jack that.

I had certainly been told to ask, 'What does the symptom mean to you?' but I had not really understood that question. What it meant was empathy. To share with a fourteen-year-old, who looked more like eleven, the hopelessness, the total, abandoned loneliness, of discovering that she was pregnant, and yet not succumb to the paralysis of pity. To enter the life of a young naval wife sufficiently to appreciate the disaster of a broken toe. Had I not had some background knowledge I would probably never have understood why she was so devastated by a relatively minor injury. She was Scottish, with no family of her own in New Zealand. Her husband was away at sea, and her only support her mother-in-law, with whom she had been battling for control of her child ever since its birth six weeks previously. This cruel blow swung the odds completely in her rival's favour.

# 13

## treatment

Among the other things to evolve over the years was my attitude to treatment. As a hospital resident fresh from medical school my approach was, 'If I want to influence the situation, I need the confidence to influence it firmly and decisively. If, for instance, I use a drug for a purpose, then I should use plenty and be sure the purpose is achieved.' I don't blame myself for thinking this way. It was, after all, the logical outcome of a mechanistic, scientific training. But it depended on the fallacies of thinking of myself and other people – other phenomena of all sorts in fact – as separate, unconnected entities, and seeing causation as a straight line from cause to effect with no feedback or interaction with other phenomena. That – as I soon discovered when I became a family doctor, later to be confirmed and amplified when I met Buddhism and, later still, general systems theory – was not how the universe really was. Far from being separate things and events, all phenomena in nature, including ourselves, were in a beautiful, dynamic balance. As I would tell my students, 'If you push nature it will push back. If you keep on pushing, it will develop a new balance which includes your push. If you then stop pushing it will tip over in the opposite direction.' The obvious example of this is the taking of tranquillizers to suppress chronic anxiety without doing anything about the underlying causes of the problem, an all-too-familiar situation in the early days of these drugs. After a time, in spite of increasing the dosage, the symptoms returned, often with the additional burden of the effects of the drugs themselves. Stopping the treatment at that point led to chaos. In hindsight, all of this is so obvious. But it is not difficult to understand how even kind, well-taught, and well-intentioned doctors, conditioned by scientific materialism, could, did, and still do, inflict untold harm on their patients.

These things were not easy to teach or to learn. In many ways, the assumptions underlying allopathic medicine conflicted with the all-embracing view of existence as total interdependence. The allopathic model was that of an observer assessing a situation objectively

69

and applying a force to change it. This implied, among other things, both disinterest and omniscience on the part of the observer, an attitude not unknown in medical people but not universally accepted, especially outside the profession. Interdependence, on the other hand, demanded I acknowledge that my cherished separateness from the universe, my very objectivity, was an illusion. No act, or even a thought, occurred in isolation. My every act influenced, to some degree, not only the process at which it was directed, but, like ripples on a pond, successive processes, which necessarily included myself. The world about me became a dynamic harmony of interacting processes. When, with due humility, I began to accept this, not only in the head but in the heart, awareness of the awful responsibility of interfering with this harmony began to dawn.

This argument was not, and is not, limited to the field of medicine. It has taken nature hundreds of millions of years to develop its present level of harmony, with its built-in checks and balances protecting its processes from harm. How arrogant is man, in his ignorance rashly manipulating the ecology in such short-sighted ways as to release self-replicating genes into environments which, having no previous experience of them, have no way of protecting themselves from harm.

To return to more familiar ground, interdependence further meant that if a medicine or any other intervention could do good, it could also do harm, unless it was applied with superhuman understanding. In medicine, as in business, there is no such thing as a free lunch. Whatever I could do to influence a dynamic balance, whether adding a chemical, manipulating, or giving advice, had consequences that spread into areas beyond my understanding. It could therefore be guaranteed free from the risk of harmful effects only if it had no effect at all, which limited its usefulness. It occurs to me now that it would be well for purveyors and consumers of all sorts of diets, herbs, medicines, procedures, and homeopathic remedies to keep this firmly in mind.

None of this denies the importance of scientific knowledge and method. What it denies is the religion called scientism, which makes science into a god of wisdom instead of a wonderfully useful but dangerous tool to be kept firmly under the control of human intelligence and morality.

From these considerations I came to question the term 'treatment', which suggests that the doctor does something to the patient in a one-way process that leaves the doctor unchanged. Perhaps, if I could avoid some of its New Age connotations, the term 'healing' would better describe what actually happens when two people interact in a clinical situation. However much the intention is that one receives help from the other, both are inevitably changed in some way. The more clearly this is recognized the more benefit is likely to result for both.

In the course of my years in medical practice I came across many drugs touted by their manufacturers as the final and complete answer to the problem, but which in the course of time turned out to be ineffective or, worse, to be positively dangerous. The most dramatic was thalidomide, the safe, non-addictive sedative, which was found years later to be responsible for major birth defects. The magical antibiotics hailed as the death of bacterial infections not only destroyed many bacterial populations that were actually beneficial to our health, but tended to become ineffective as bacteria learned to be resistant to them. Then there were the tranquillizers that were to solve problems of anxiety, only to become objects of addiction. The list went on. And behind the whole problem lay the wish to have something for nothing, to have perfection from a bottle, combined with the arrogance that believed it could ride roughshod over the dynamic balances of nature.

# 14

# lighter moments

Rain. My introduction to the North Shore, in those days a rather inaccessible suburb of Auckland, occurred in February 1959. I arrived at Devonport by vehicular ferry in a tropical downpour, my new Rover 90 packed with wife (suffering from pregnancy sickness), child (15 months old, tired, hungry, and fractious), and all our possessions. Recalling that drive through Victoria Street – with a river rushing down the hill towards me, threatening to engulf the car and all I valued – I can hear again the voice in the back of my head: 'What possessed you to bring your family from that safe cottage in an English village to come to this?'

More rain. Only a week or two later I answered my first night call to a private house in another downpour. It was at the far end of Nile Road; well named, I thought. As the trusty Rover surged along, I stopped at each standing wave to wade ahead, prodding the road with an umbrella to be sure it had not been washed away. Again I wondered, 'Why did I decide this was the life for me?' But I knew really. The pioneering spirit was strangled in London. This sort of challenge was what life was all about.

So many skills I had not discovered. One of them was the art of syringing wax from a blocked ear. It looked easy enough, and when the large and truculent local policeman presented his blocked ears one evening, I wielded the syringe with a will. What nobody had pointed out to me was that if the water is not close to body temperature, it may irritate the balance organ and cause dizziness and even vomiting. It did. As my patient lay retching on the floor, it occurred to me that it was time I thought of an urgent matter that needed my attention elsewhere. On another occasion, as I aimed a jet of carefully warmed water into the ear of an Irish navvy he clapped his hand firmly over the other ear. I still don't know if this was a reflex action or a calculated joke.

Ruling the practice with a firm hand was Margaret, the practice nurse. Margaret, from Yorkshire, insisted that she would never forgive me for asking her on our first meeting if she was from Lancashire. She was a fountain of knowledge about the district and its people, who paid their fees and who didn't, who was having an affair with whom, and, above all, who I must never allow an evening appointment, as there was no nurse or female receptionist to act as chaperone. This list was headed by Ruth, whom I had already met and examined, closely attended by Margaret, before whom nobody would risk anything untoward. I only half believed this tale, and when Ruth phoned one evening complaining of dreadful abdominal pains, which from her description sounded very like appendicitis, I invited her to the consulting room. I thought it was probably safer to examine her on my territory than on hers, but I could not forget the horror stories about women tearing their clothes and threatening to scream if handsome payment was not immediately forthcoming. Ruth certainly did not look sick when she swept into my room. In fact she looked, and smelt, ravishing. Having accepted the invitation to go behind the curtain and lie on the examination couch, she promptly emerged wearing nothing but the flimsiest of underwear and advanced towards me, blocking my escape. Fortunately there was enough room to squeeze past the west end of my desk, as Ruth advanced from the east, and escape to the safety of the waiting room. After engaging the next patient in conversation for a few minutes I cautiously returned to the consulting room, leaving the door ajar. By this time Ruth had accepted defeat, dressed, and with a charming smile took her departure. Whenever I met her in the street in the years to come I was greeted with the same dazzling smile. It was good to know there were no hard feelings.

Ailsa was a beautiful woman, fair of complexion, tall, and in spite of having two children, both of whom I had delivered, of firm and shapely figure. She phoned me one day and, quite uncharacteristically, asked me to call to see her at home. She hesitantly explained that although she wasn't very ill, she had sore throat and a rash that she was afraid to show in public. It was a steamy February day. Ailsa was lying on her bed, clad only in a flimsy nightgown, which at the appropriate moment she pulled up to her neck, to expose a scarlet fever rash of text-book perfection. 'My, isn't that beautiful!' I gasped. After a shocked pause we both burst into slightly embarrassed laughter. I hastened to explain that scarlet fever, especially demonstrating so perfectly the myriad tiny, bright red spots on a paler red background, was at this point in history quite rare. But the damage was done, and the story had spread round the district almost before I had regained the safety of the surgery.

I had known Rowley and Helen for some years, through preg-
nancies, deliveries, and Helen's asthma. Until the present incident,
Rowley had been a spectator of matters medical. It was just before
dawn on a summer's morning when Helen phoned to say that Rowley
was in the most dreadful pain. A few quick questions and the sound of
Rowley's groans in the background established that he had the
dreaded colic, caused by a small stone passing from kidney to bladder.
As I arrived at the house Helen flung open the front door and stood in
her nightgown, silhouetted by the hall light, urging me to hurry. Perhaps I was affected by her urgency, or possibly dazzled by the light. My
toe struck the top step and I fell on top of the now prostrate Helen in
the hallway, just as the milk delivery truck pulled up behind my car.
That tale also did the rounds.

The clifftop where we bought a piece of unpromising-looking
scrub-covered clay on which to build a house and raise a family, faced
north towards the Auckland shipping lane. This was also the expected
approach of the Japanese during the invasion threat of 1944. As was
proper under the circumstances, the army had occupied some nearby
parkland on which it set up three big guns, one of which, according to
legend, was once fired. So many windows in the neighbourhood were
shattered, so the story goes, that it was never fired again. By the time
of this story, the guns had long gone, but not so the nearby accommodation: hastily built bungalows, which from their size suggested that
army officers were a fecund lot. Many-roomed houses, now owned by
the local town council and let for small rentals, attracted a colourful
and multi-coloured population to what was otherwise an exclusive
area. Many were my adventures in and around these houses.

One of them was occupied by Mrs Mac and a remaining unmar-
ried son. Mrs Mac was a Scot, nearly six feet tall, weighing some 250
pounds, and in spite of most of a lifetime spent in New Zealand, pre-
served a mostly unintelligible Glaswegian accent. Mrs Mac was also
diabetic, and so bitterly opposed to syringes and needles that she
managed to have insulin overdose comas in an astonishing variety of
inconvenient places. The one that sticks in my mind took place in a
toilet – whose door opened inwards. 250 pounds of inert body
slumped against a locked door posed a problem not anticipated by
the learned teachers of 'diabetes and its complications'. The lock having yielded to a broom-handle poked through the window, the son, a
taciturn but massive young man, was able, with feet on the door and
back against the wall on the other side of the corridor, to move the

door a few inches and expose an unidentified part of his mother's anatomy. Into this I thrust an injection of adrenaline which, to our delight and my surprise, roused Mrs Mac enough to allow her to heave herself away from the door and back onto the seat.

One morning during an intense consultation I was annoyed to hear the buzz from the office that told me I had to answer the phone. The receptionist's voice was hesitant but insistent. 'It's Charles from Castor Bay Road. He says you have to visit. I told him you wouldn't go to his place again since his dog bit you but he says it's urgent.' Then Charles himself, 'Doc, I'm crook.' 'What sort of crook, Charles?' 'Crook in the guts, Doc. Jeez, Doc, you know what it's like to be crook in the guts. I'm gonna bloody die, Doc, if you don't get here soon. Dog's tied up, Doc, I promise.' He sounded sick – and he had a duodenal ulcer, which in my imagination had perforated and was at this moment pumping gastric acid into his peritoneum. Reluctantly, fearfully, I took myself to Charles's house, vividly recalling the visit during which an Alsatian had bitten me severely on the leg as I negotiated the precipitous path down to the front door. There was the dog, as big as a donkey, and there, reassuringly, was a massive chain attached to its collar. What I didn't know was that the chain was long enough to reach the door. Just as my hand reached the handle there was a thump on both shoulders and heavy, halitotic panting in my ear. I stood paralysed with fear, imagining being decapitated by a playful bite, or at least losing an ear. Eventually, in response to a loud groan from inside, the dog jumped down and watched me suspiciously, threateningly, as I edged through the door. Charles's ulcer had not perforated. It was merely suffering the consequences of being bathed in quantities of poor whisky, which was fortunate for both of us. I have wondered since then how I would have escaped, or how we would have carried Charles out past the dog, had he not been able to rise from his bed to explain the situation to the creature.

Down in Craig Road, alongside the beach, ran a row of dilapidated houses, in one of which lived Mrs Clark, an elderly lady whose dress and habits my nurse described as 'idiosyncratic'. There was something about old Mrs Clark that I found attractive. In fact I was very fond of her. So when she rang in the early hours of a morning to tell me she was having a heart attack, that she wanted me to come, but that she would not go to hospital, there was no electricity because she had not paid the bill, and that I would have to climb in the window nearest to the front door, I went willingly. What she did not tell me was that she shared the house with eleven chihuahuas, each of was intent on sacrificing its life to protect its mistress. As my exploring foot reached down into the darkness from the window sill, a hundred needle-sharp teeth sank themselves into my trousers, fortunately heavy tweed since it was a cold night. By torchlight I dragged a pile of tiny dogs to the bedroom door, whereupon they detached themselves to scramble onto the bed and surround their mistress with a ring of defensive teeth. In the dim light it was not easy to operate my clumsy, battery-operated cardiograph with eleven aggressive dogs tangling themselves in the wires. But the diagnosis was eventually confirmed, a large anterior cardiac infarct seriously threatening her life. 'Thank you, doctor. A little morphine would be nice, and would you come back in the morning to see if I'm alive? It's good to know you can now write a death certificate if I'm not.' So back to bed. She was alive in the morning, and for a number of years after that, in spite of her refusal of any help except a little shopping and some occasional token house-work from a neighbour.

Not all the threats came from patients and their dogs. By the time I came to move to a small house to live alone, I had been in prac-tice for twenty-five years, long enough to have met and survived all possible dangers, or so I thought. One of the attractions of my new house was a flourishing rose garden, in the middle of which stood a blue moon, a sturdy bush with a large, pale blue blooms. The colour was so intriguing that I took the first opening bud of the summer to grace my desk. I discovered my mistake within half an hour. As well as a most unusual colour, blue moon had a delicate but penetrating scent that excited my dormant hay fever into paroxysms of sneezing. I innocently took the beautiful but offending bloom to the office and offered it to the new receptionist, with the suggestion that it would look lovely on her desk. Months later, when we knew each other much better, she confessed that she had sought legal advice on suing me for sexual harassment.

# 15

# death

I was not in practice very long before I met Death.

Death was the end, the ultimate failure. When I met my patients and their problems it was absolutely necessary that I did something useful for them. Take Barbara, for instance. Barbara, small, modest, loyal, who never breathed word of criticism or blame. Barbara, aged 30, with two children and a modest little husband, had belly aches and some diarrhoea. Who wouldn't, with her drab, dull life of struggling to make ends meet? Ian drove heavy machines all day, shifting mountains of clay and rubble, while Barbara held the family together. What she needed was kindness and sympathy, and that was what I most liked to give. But her belly began to blow up, and I had to see she had a bowel obstruction. It couldn't be large bowel cancer in a woman of thirty with no relevant family history. But it could, and was. Furthermore, it had seeded through liver and omentum. It was my fault that Barbara was going to die slowly and miserably, leaving Ian and the children without help, support, and stability.

The cancer spread. She developed a lump under the skin of the belly, near the colostomy. Then another, and another, until her trunk and even her limbs were covered with little lumps under the skin – growing – breeding – and it was all my fault. Pain from cancerous growths. Vomiting. Misery, but never a complaint. Did I see accusation in those deep-sunk eyes? Of course I saw it, but did Barbara put it there or did I? Vomiting. Couldn't swallow morphine. Ian couldn't face giving Barbara injections, so I eased my guilt by calling several times a day to give her the morphine she needed.

Barbara took months to die, fading very slowly, becoming jaundiced, then the dreadful lime-green of liver failure. Still she lingered, to look at me with those eyes that got bigger as her body shrank away. Always, 'Thank you, doctor, you are so very kind.' And another arrow pierced my guilty heart because I hadn't suspected early enough to save her life.

So to the inevitable failure, and Barbara's death. I had failed to save her life, medical science had failed, even the devoted Ian had failed. Barbara was dead. No longer was I to be reminded of my failure several times a day. Now I could bury it deep – but not before I had wept long and loud in self-pity – deep, deep down where the black, stinking knowledge that I was no good, worthy of rejection by all who would love me, could lurk out of sight.

Such was death to me as a newly qualified medico, practising alone after five years of protection by the hospital hierarchy. Nobody had led me to know that death was just another change. All the animals I had killed in my youth had not taught me. Nothing could have penetrated my perfectionism at that stage of my life.

Death was to be denied. When I, the doctor, could no longer cure, I stepped aside and let people of religion offer what pale comfort they could.

Could nobody have helped me to know that death is? That death not only is, but is OK? That it is the ordinary end to this earthly life; that it has a place that not only can't be escaped from, but which contains the meaning and purpose of life? How much misery I could have avoided for myself, and for my dying patients and their families, if I could have known in my guts that death is OK.

From many years afterwards, I could not possibly have accepted that death is OK while I knew that in order to be OK myself I had to succeed, and that the doctor's role was to cure. What a catch-22 to be in!

How did I react? With resignation, as my father had taught me. Without complaint, to resign myself to knowing that sooner or later I was to fail to prevent the death of every single person I met. And, to my present disbelief, that is where I stayed, year after year, working for diagnosis and cure, seeing every success as real and permanent, and resigning myself to the guilt of failure when death came.

The process of coming to terms with death evolved over the thirty years of my life as a family doctor, and for my subsequent years as a Buddhist. Through all the many ways individuals met their death, I met my own fears and denials.

I must have been in practice for about three years when my mother phoned me late one evening. Her voice was anxious, which was nothing unusual, but her request was urgent and fearful. 'I'm worried about Dad. Can you come and see him?' 'Do you mean now?' We lived some 400 kilometres apart, all of five hours' drive. 'Well, as soon as you can. He can't swallow properly, and he won't go and tell the doctor about it.'

When I last saw him, about a year previously, my father had been a vigorous 75-year-old, amusing himself by breeding rare breeds of sheep on a small farm. Two days after my mother's phone call I met a very different man. His efforts to hide his difficulty in swallowing soon broke down, and before long we were discussing the obstruction in his gullet. The following day, a barium swallow confirmed that he had a cancer causing an almost complete blockage at the junction of gullet and stomach. Totally dispassionately, as befitting two reasonable men, we discussed his options. There was but one lapse into emotion when in a voice of gentle exasperation he muttered, 'It took me until two years ago to discover that there was more to life than working, and now I've got this damned cancer!' Finally he stood up with, 'Well, my boy, I've got some interesting things to do if I can live a bit longer. I want this thing treated.'

Two days later the discussion was resumed in David Cole's office in the Cardio-thoracic Surgical Unit at Green Lane Hospital. David spelled out the options while I explained them in the special voice I'd developed to penetrate Father's deafness thirty years previously. The operation was still not much past the experimental stage. First, to build a new gullet, using a length of large bowel drawn up behind the breast bone, then perhaps, at a later date, to try to remove the cancer.

Characteristically decisive (his deafness had trained him to act on first information without the benefit of qualifying clauses), Father stood up and pronounced, 'I've got nothing to lose. I'll trade the few miserable weeks I would have without the operation for a chance to be well for a while. But no half measures. I want to be dead or pretty fit!'

He made a remarkable recovery from what seemed to me horrific surgery. During those weeks between the operations he lived with my sister a short distance from my home, and frequently came with me on my house calls. We both knew his time was short. Although he looked and felt well, the cancer had been found to have penetrated the pericardium, and would soon be causing major trouble with his heart. One day he said, 'I still want to be well enough to go home for a while. I'm going to ask David if he can cut this cancer out and give me a bit longer. But before I do that, tell me, what was my life for?'

What was his life for? What was my life for? What was anybody's life for? People just didn't ask questions like that. It was embarrassing.

So nobody, at least nobody in medical circles, talked about it. I started to talk about his achievements, but he cut me short, 'Yes, I know about all that, but now I'm dying it doesn't count for much. There must be more to it than that.' There must indeed, but not in my experience. 'Oh well,' he said, 'it was worth a try. I thought you might have some good ideas.'

He had the second operation and, not unexpectedly, died a few days later. His last words to me were, 'I'm not going to make it, my boy, but young David's learned a thing or two.'

I was not with him when he died. Neither were my mother or my sister, or either of my two brothers, though there seem to have been no good reasons why we could not have been there. It just was not done to interrupt one's life to sit uselessly by while a relative died. He was not conscious, so we couldn't do anything to help. It was an old classmate of mine who phoned to say he was dead. When I thanked him for his kindness, he said, 'I must say, you're taking this very well,' to which I replied, 'There's no point in taking it any other way.'

I didn't mourn for my father, not because of any great effort to keep a stiff upper lip, but because I felt no grief. I saw his body only momentarily, for official identification. During the funeral ceremony, conducted by a strange priest, the coffin was tightly sealed. 'And well it might be,' my brother remarked. 'He wouldn't have had much time for all that religious mumbo-jumbo.' There was a moment of awareness of an odd sensation in my chest as the coffin began to sink discretely from sight, but nothing to distract me from seeing that my mother was OK before I went back to work. It was many years before I really experienced and came to terms with my father's death.

Some years later I met George, or the Major, as he still pictured himself. He was walking one day by the sea with his wife, when he jumped from one rock to another, and fell to the ground with a broken femur. 'Must have fainted or something,' he said indignantly. 'I don't remember falling hard enough to break anything. Just seemed to break as I jumped.'

Had I listened to George as he spoke – had I really heard the surprise and indignation in his voice and been less impressed with what looked on the X-ray like an ordinary fractured neck of the femur – I would have realized the truth much earlier. But the fracture healed after being fixed wth a nail, and it was not for some months that it became obvious that George had a cancer of the prostate with secondary growths in many bones. The bone that 'just seemed to break' as he jumped, was now the site of a big lump of cancer tissue.

This was one of the prostate cancers that did not respond to hormones. The Major – I don't think he ever accepted that he was George to me – followed a rapid course of what looked like accelerated ageing, becoming more and more shrunken and shrivelled day by day. But until the moment he died, George denied that death was coming. He flatly refused to consider the possibility that he wouldn't be walking again next week. He would have none of making his peace with his daughter, who desperately sought reconciliation from some long-passed hurt. 'Plenty of time for that when I'm well again,' was the best we could get from him.

I think I was as deeply affected by George's death as I was by Barbara's, not, this time, because of my own real or imagined failings, but by the sense of a life wasted. His approaching death was not all that George had denied. He had denied his very existence as a human being, and apart from the achievement of having made his bit of the army operate smoothly, he might just as well never have lived. Of course, what I was really mourning was my own life denied. Another lesson in the learning.

I was privileged to meet Emily the day she was expected to die. So much of her body had been taken over by the cancer; so little left to house continuing life. Her cancer had blocked her common bile duct. For weeks, her colour had deepened into the muddy yellow of chronic jaundice, then the deep olive green that few people live long enough to reach.

'I am so tired,' she told me. 'I want to die now, not wait any longer, but the girls won't let me.' The girls were her two daughters, both in their thirties, who had come over from Australia to be with their mother when she died. I discussed with them the possibility of just letting their mother go. At first it was denial, disbelief, then open refusal, then, ever so slowly, amid the tears of all the grief they had never allowed to be felt, acceptance. All this took several days, while Emily patiently waited. Only then were we able to sit with Emily while her two daughters and their father, and finally I, assured her that we were OK now. It was all right for her to go.

Emily went to sleep that night and quietly ceased breathing. She was a Christian with little regard for the dogma of the Roman Catholic Church within which she was raised. She knew about love, and about Jesus as its messenger, and needed no more. She was quite content with not knowing what she would meet when she let go of her worn-out body, but, enveloped in her awareness of love, she quietly and courageously moved to meet it.

I became very fond of Emily in the few days that I knew her. By this time I had moved a long way towards acknowledging and overcoming my own fear of death, and I felt Emily's longing for release as if it were my own. Her love was more deeply developed than mine. I managed my resentment of her daughters' refusal to release her less skilfully than she did. She was a lesson in love.

Her death moved me to an unexpected and profound joy – a sense of taking part in a life completed, and – although I had not yet met Buddhism and the doctrine of re-becoming – a feeling of new life beginning. At the very least I had experienced death as a natural and positive event, a completion rather than a failure. Grief, too, was natural, to be accepted, experienced as part of living. I even had the first faint awareness that grief in itself was not truly painful. That the pain was in denial, and that grief accepted in full awareness had a quality of expansiveness, of love, even of what I was later to recognize as the sublime emotion of *metta*, the undiscriminating love for all beings.

By the time I met Angus I thought I had this death thing by the tail. A surgeon to whom I had often referred patients rang to ask me to drop in on an old friend of his who had a massive cancer in his pelvis. 'Retired GP from the country,' he said, 'Salt of the earth. Can't do anything. Just pain relief.' I was met at the door by Angus's wife, who hurried me into the garden out of the patient's hearing. 'Don't talk to him about death. Of course he knows he's dying, but he's never talked about death. It's too late to change that now.' It wasn't too late, although it took many visits and some hours of conversation before I felt it was time to raise the subject. No sooner had Angus admitted he was dying and begun to give directions for his funeral at the marae where he had been in practice for so many years, than both ureters were taken over by the cancer. He had only a day or two of lucidity before the waste products would build up in his blood to cloud consciousness, then lead to coma and death. The relief of being able to share his loneliness and fear switched him from brooding silence to enthusiasm for sharing his experience, even to jocularity. What a privilege it was to sit and share his vast experience of life and death as his own death crept up on him. Among other things, I learned that I still had much to learn.

In the last year of my life as a family doctor, I was fortunate enough to meet Harry. He was something over 80 when I met him, a retired retailer from a country town, who had moved to the city to be near his family. Harry and his wife Anne had that rare and sublime friendship that sometimes occurs to confound the cynics. In their new environment they settled down to enjoy their last few years together. They worked to build a garden – Harry's interest was in roses and his wife's in various shrubs and blooms – and together they joined the local bowling club. Harry also played a little golf, and it was on the golf course that I first met him.

One day, Harry made an appointment to tell me of his breathlessness and cough. He had a cancer of the lung which had already destroyed what little lung tissue he had in reserve, and was now invading the lymph nodes in the centre of his chest. He had not timed it well for our relationship. I had just arranged to take three months off to go to Britain for some first-hand information about the Friends of the Western Buddhist Order. I had almost decided that it was time to move the centre of my life from medicine to Buddhism. All I needed was information and the courage to make the move.

'Pity about that,' was his comment. 'I would have liked you to be there when I die.' After checking with his wife and family, Harry decided not to have any treatment, but to enter his last bowls tournament without telling anybody else about his cancer.

Poor Harry. The tournament was going well when a few weeks later he dropped dead on the bowling green. He was well prepared for death. What he was not prepared for was waking up in hospital after being resuscitated by an enthusiastic first aid worker. His sense of humour almost met the situation, but not quite. When I returned from my travels it was to meet an indignant Harry being bundled into an ambulance and taken to the hospital for radiotherapy. Taking courage from my presence, he politely cancelled the next hospital appointment and went back to his roses.

Not long afterwards, Anne phoned me to say that Harry had gone. There he was, lying on his lawn, a rose and his secateurs beside him. Nobody was going to try to resuscitate him this time. With her daughter's help, Anne and I carried him to his bed – there wasn't much of him by this time – and together we wept a tear for a departed friend. I was able to whisper a few words of reassurance to him, to tell him that he was dead, that his loved ones were ready to let him go, and to wish him well on his journey. As the three of us stood hand in hand, speaking our farewells in turn, my mind went back to so many deaths I had seen so badly managed, and I rejoiced for all of us. I rejoiced especially for my own acceptance of death after so many years of the pain of denial, and for my good fortune in meeting a teacher such as Harry at the end of my medical career.

My association with medicine was over, but not with death. With the passing years, more of my acquaintances and friends were meeting cancer, coronary artery disease, and all the problems of ageing bodies wearing out. I had been back in New Zealand as a member of the Western Buddhist Order for some years before I met Brian. His son, Guhyasiddhi, a fellow member of the Order with whom I shared a community house, introduced us in the hope that we would have something to share. We soon found that we shared a passionate love for the New Zealand bush, for wild and lonely places on the coast, in fact for natural beauty wherever we could find it. The formation of new friendships is not easy for older people. Habits become fixed, and innovations like admitting a new person to one's life can be major hurdles. However, sharing what we were both thoroughly familiar with, the tracks and beaches of this beautiful land, carried us through the initial resistance to the development of a deep friendship.

It was on the morning of Good Friday, while I was on a meditation retreat, that Guhyasiddhi phoned me. 'I thought you should know that Dad died last night. He was doing his lengths in the swimming pool and his heart stopped.' 'No!' I thought aloud, 'Not Brian! We're going walking next week as usual. He can't be dead!' But, yes, it was Brian, and he was dead. He had survived a heart attack some years before, but this was one more than his tired, old heart could stand. As disbelief faded, the sensation familiar from the pains of childhood grew in my chest; the hot, prickling, nauseated sensation behind the middle of the breast bone that I later identified as the choking of suppressed weeping, as denied grief. Carefully replacing the telephone, I walked slowly, deliberately, so as not to disturb the other retreatants, away from the dining room down to the lonely coast where the flood burst. The tears were not for Brian. He had what he had wanted, death from a state of activity, avoiding what he most feared, being alive but unable to walk in the bush. The unrestrained weeping was for myself and for his family. For the first time I knew in the depth of my heart that the death of one we love is loss, the tearing away of what we most value. And the natural response to loss is grief, whose expression is weeping. Why did I weep so long for the loss of that old man whom I had known for only a few years? I wept not only for him but for all the other loss in my life whose grief I had been unable to experience fully; the loss of a pet lamb, of the dog that had transferred her allegiance when I left her to go to boarding school, of Christine my first love, and of my father, especially of my father nearly forty years previously.

That evening I again spoke with Guhyasiddhi on the phone. 'We would like you to conduct the death ceremony,' he told me. I had led several such ceremonies for others, but never for anybody as close to me as Brian.

'I would be honoured, but I may not be able to keep my dignity.'

'Don't worry about that. We won't either!'

Leading that ceremony was a deeply moving experience. 'We are here,' I told the assembled gathering, 'to rejoice in Brian's life, to acknowledge and share our grief, to support Brian in his present journey, wherever that may be, and to use the presence of death to reflect on our own death and make our lives more meaningful.' I heard many of his friends and family speak of the man they knew, and myself spoke of the Brian that I knew. Guhyasiddhi and I chanted a mantra as the coffin slid smoothly from sight. The following day I kept the appointment in my diary, to walk with Brian through the forest to a grove of majestic kauri trees. So strongly could I feel his presence beside me that I expected at any moment to see him and hear his voice. There I left him, his face upturned to the trees we both loved so deeply, his hands folded on the top of his walking stick, to walk home alone.

Death comes ever nearer. Ralph, while working on his farm at the tender age of 76, suffered a stroke that destroyed a small but essential piece of his brain. Assured by the experts that he would never again open his eyes, swallow, speak, or walk, and that removal of the life support would lead to his death within a day or two, I joined with our sister Mary Rose and Ralph's daughter and two sons to make the dreadful decision to do just that. He refused to die, and now lives a half-life in a nursing home, seeing, swallowing, and walking but too seriously impaired to return to a more independent life.

A few weeks later Mary Rose, a vigorous eighty-one, complained of clumsiness in her left hand. The following day her physician invited me to look at her brain scan. There on the screen was the dense shadow of an invasive tumour as big as a golf ball, deep in her right brain. I quote from a letter to the Western Buddhist Order journal of a few months later.

> Mary Rose died three days ago, less than four months from the first symptom of a brain cancer. My daughter Ayla and I promised her in early January that with the help of professional caregivers we would keep her in her own house as long as we could provide what she needed. It was a big job, but we did it, and were with her when she took her last breath. It's been a time of intense learning for me. The pre-dawn hours of sitting beside a woman who has been a close companion and friend for a long time as she slipped in and out of consciousness have been so productive of deepening reflection. Often as I watched her level of consciousness fluctuating, reflections would start. Where is she now? Where will she be when the gaps in the breathing extend from ten or fifteen seconds to a minute, an hour, or a day? Who is she now? Who will she be when breathing stops? And so to reflection on the nature of life and death, of the sense of identity now and after the body dies. Many new little insights and an ever deepening sense of mystery.

I conducted her death ceremony too, this time surrounded by my own family and friends, then went away to the family cottage at Kawau Island for a few days to assimilate the intense experiences of the previous few months.

So many deaths, over so many years. Now, increasingly, it is my death that interests me. There have been 'little deaths', becoming more important as I grow older. The death of the man who could climb cliffs and crash through the bush without thought of accident or injury. A torn shoulder capsule from a fall, months of increasing pain, and major repair surgery left me restricted. Only slightly limited physically, but now and hereafter cautious, never able to forget for long that I could so easily be injured, helpless, and alone in some remote gully in a bush-clad range. So the new, cautious man keeps to tracks and carries an emergency locator beacon.

The death of the Provider, the driving, driven man taking responsibility for getting things done, about whom more will be said in chapter 23, to be reborn as a gentler, more contemplative man, seeking appreciative understanding of the universe rather than trying to remodel it to his own design. The daily death of who I was yesterday, to re-become as I am today, according to the Buddhist teaching, 'neither the same nor different'.

It is this new man who thinks of death. Thinks of the times he has meditated beside the open coffin of a dead friend, and the insights that have arisen. Thinks of those dead friends with gratitude for their gifts of understanding. Thinks how much more effective those gifts would have been if death had not been so sanitized with make-up, formal dress, and shiny, veneered coffins with silver handles. How can I most effectively perform this last service for my friends? By appearing to them as myself dead. Which suggests that my body should be dressed in familiar clothes, lying in a plain wooden box which I have made for myself.

So much for physical death, but what of the stream of conscious events that I call 'me'? By joyfully contemplating giving the body that I no longer need as an object of contemplation for my friends, do I overlook the fate of that stream of consciousness? Am I in fact falling into the trap of nihilism, the belief that nothing continues beyond physical death? If so, there is work to be done. Nihilism and eternalism - belief in a permanent, unchanging soul - are the two great 'wrong views' that Buddhists strive to overcome.

Buddhism tells me firmly that 'I' comprise no more than a stream of mind states, each arising in dependence on previous states; that nowhere is there a permanent, unchanging thing I can identify as a self. That's all very well, but it is not how I live. At this moment, as I sit overlooking Tararu Valley, a multitude of birdsong backed by the ever-present murmur of a waterfall, feeling the cool, southerly breeze on my face, 'I' am. I most certainly exist. To say otherwise would be just silly. On my present level of consciousness, not only do I exist, but so do the birds, the trees, and the stone on which I stub my toe. Each exists as a separate and apparently unchanging entity.

If there is but one ultimate reality – and there can be only one – how can this be? It must have something to do with changing levels of perception. On my present level of consciousness, reality is relative, tentative, changing with each piece of new evidence. On the level of the Enlightened mind, ultimate reality is complete, unchanging, inconceivable, and so indescribable. In my present experience I exist as a separate being. Assuming that I don't attain Insight in the meantime, I will still seem to have a separate existence at the time of my physical death.

Now for an exercise in imagination. As my consciousness leaves the confines of the physical body, it will presumably continue to see itself as a separate entity. According to the *Tibetan Book of the Dead*, a traditional Tibetan Buddhist text, someone who has recently died finds it difficult to accept they are dead, and continues to experience a body, albeit a subtle, non-material one. (I am surprised that I find this idea so strange, since I experience myself in a non-material body in dreams.) And there is no reason to suppose that I will shed the illusion of selfhood just because I have discarded my physical body.

Let imagination follow my journey through the death *bardo*, the state of existence between one life and another. Confined within a body ruled by its sensory needs, I could not meet the truth that threatened my cherished (perceived) self. But freed from physical restriction, I find myself faced with ultimate reality. Now follows a frantic search for familiarity, in which my ability to perceive reality becomes progressively obscured. Eventually I find a level familiar enough to reach for. So 'I' am reborn. From one life, through the *bardo*, to the next, I have carried the illusion of a fixed self. That is what is reborn. On the level of ultimate reality, what makes that journey is nothing but a series of mind states, each arising in dependence on previous mind states. But that to me is an abstract idea which cannot become truth until my consciousness has expanded so far as to know it as direct experience.

The *Tibetan Book of the Dead* also convincingly assures us that this *bardo* state offers us great opportunities to expand our state of consciousness, but that is another story.

To return to the accusation of nihilism. I must forgive myself if, momentarily, I allow my present earth-bound mind to imagine death in earth-bound terms – as the end of experience. But imagination needs only a moment's effort to know that, while the experience of the senses ends, all subtler forms of experience continue. Why should they not?

# 16

# finding the way

I don't remember how I came to be helping my sister Mary sort out her old books in the spring of 1982. Or why I should have been so struck by a battered book on Buddhism (unless it was the unusual name of the author, Christmas Humphreys) as to take it home with me and start reading it in bed that night. On the first page I began to read about the Four Noble Truths: that this life can never be completely satisfactory; that this is because of craving, always wanting things to be different (even convincing ourselves that they are different) from how they are; that if we could overcome this discontent we would overcome the essential unsatisfactoriness of life; and that we can achieve this by following the Noble Eightfold Path. As the argument unravelled the first two of these propositions, I felt the rising excitement. All the confusions, tangles, and dead-ends of thirty years of searching were being picked up, sorted out, and pieced together by clear vision and thought. This was important, urgent, not a time for sleeping. Page followed page. Yes, of course! That's how it is. Why had I never seen it before? The third proposition was obvious enough. All religious teachers said that sort of thing. If you put aside your desire for the pleasures of the senses, you open the path to heaven. Of course, but how? You can't just walk away from desires as though discarding a worn-out shirt. They are stuck firmly to your back and won't come off. And there for all to see, in the fourth statement, was exactly how to go about it, spelled out in clear, simple terms. This was what was so different. This book on Buddhism was telling me not only what I should do to overcome discontent, it was telling me precisely how I could do it, by my own efforts. I did not have to take on any bundle of impossible beliefs, or pray to a God I knew didn't exist. All I needed was the desire to change, and the tools were right there waiting for me. Within an hour or two I knew I was a Buddhist and always had been. It had taken all those years of fumbling about in the dark to prepare me for this, to make me receptive to the Dharma, the teaching of the Buddha, when it was offered to me.

There I was, in the early hours of the morning, a convinced Buddhist; but also a family doctor with a wife and five children, living and working in an affluent and conservative suburb of Auckland in the late twentieth century. As far as I knew, Buddhism as an active force had died out long ago in Asia, and had never been taken up in Europe except by a few enthusiasts like Christmas Humphreys. There was obviously no way I could practise Buddhism in public, in Auckland. Not in my situation. It would never do. But there were books.

As I was soon to discover, there *were* books, lots of books. There were academic treatises by learned authors like Humphreys, there were translations into stilted and largely unintelligible English of Sanskrit and Pali texts, and there were mountains of books with enigmatic titles by American converts to Zen and various Tibetan traditions. It was these last that I found most confusing. How the challenging teaching of the Buddha translated into these New Age, flower-power terms I completely failed to understand. In fact I strongly suspected that some of the authors had merely suppressed their discomfort and continued to write in spite of a similar failure. (It was not until some years later that I discovered that to change oneself deep down rather than merely change one's ideas, to become the progressively different person that the spiritual life demands, requires prolonged contact with a teacher, someone who is actively changing by constant practice.)

After about two years of wandering around in this maze of words, on a blustery Wednesday afternoon in mid-October, I was enjoying a round of golf. We were half way down the fifteenth fairway, in fact, where big pine trees throw a blue shadow on bright spring grass, when, with no warning at all, my partner Colin suddenly said, 'Do you have a religion?' We usually didn't have time for that sort of conversation among our complaints about the state of the greens and the iniquities of our fellow club members. Besides which, conversation was generally reserved for the walk between strokes, not times such as this, when I was weighing the merits of a 3-iron against a 4-wood for the crucial second into the wind. Colin's question so took me by surprise that I answered honestly, 'I'm a Buddhist.' 'That's interesting,' he said. 'Do you worship with those Tibetans out at Kaukapakapa?' Of course I didn't worship with anybody – I just read the books and thought about things. Suddenly I was lonely. Something in me needed to move from being an observer on the sidelines, to go out on the field and do this thing, to become it, whatever it was. I had to find some Buddhists, even if they were strange academics or shaven-headed monks.

Where to seek? Of course, the telephone book. Not a single entry under 'Buddhist'. Well, that settles that, there aren't any of them after all. But the niggling little voice was not to be quieted. The *Yellow Pages*: Religious Institutions. There it was, Auckland Buddhist Centre. 'It will be quite safe to phone them,' I thought, 'I won't have to go there'. Nothing I had read to date had dispelled my notion that real Buddhists were monks with yellow robes, shaven heads, and incense who lived on alms provided by the gullible public. After all, I was a pillar of society, a picture of respectability. It wouldn't do to be seen in the company of a bunch of odd-looking layabouts who didn't work for their living.

As I dialled the number with clammy fingers I had a clear picture in my mind of an ancient Asian, none too clean, groping through a cloud of incense for the phone and muttering unintelligibly. 'Hello. This is the Auckland Buddhist Centre.' It was a woman, for goodness sake, a young one, and a New Zealander at that.

'Oh, er, I seem to be some sort of a Buddhist and I want to meet some Buddhists,' 'Oh, that's nice,' said the cheerful voice. 'Why don't you come round on Tuesday evening and see what we look like?' See what *we* look like. She was one of them. No monk I ever imagined had a voice like that. The voice went on, 'I'll meet you there. My name is Vidyavati.' She spelled it out for me, gave me an address, and changed the course of my life.

Since that night I have often marvelled at what a slender thread my spiritual life hung on at that moment. Had the response to my first hesitant contact been less positive, I could so easily have not gone 'round on Tuesday evening'. And had I chanced on a different Buddhist movement I could so easily have failed to make a connection.

And so it was that, dragging Mary along for support (after all it was her book that had started this), I arrived that Tuesday evening in October 1984, at the Hobson Street Centre. Vidyavati, at first meeting, was a delight. Attractive in a bright summer frock, intelligent, interested, with a rare, relaxed friendliness. I can still feel the extraordinary atmosphere that met me as I went into that room. There were fifteen or twenty people present, chatting and drinking tea. Vidyavati and some others wore broad bands of white ribbon round their necks. One of these, who said his name was Purna, offered me a cup of tea with, 'You can't be a Buddhist if you don't drink tea.' Later he showed me how to sit on a meditation stool, which was the only meditation instruction on offer that evening. There was something quite unusual about this gathering. A vague reminder of my first meeting with an Alcoholics Anonymous group: the natural acceptance of me, a stranger. But it was much deeper than that. These people were really, genuinely friendly, not only to me, but to one another. And in a quiet way they were happy – and peaceful. The whole room breathed friendship. Not the cloying, clinging friendship of an evangelical group, but genuine warmth – dare I say love?

My ear caught a conversation. Two people discussing a third…. Now this was different. These people were sharing their joy at the other person's success in some pursuit that I don't remember, if I ever heard it. But they were really happy about it. Of all the memories of that evening, my introduction to the Friends of the Western Buddhist Order, a few stand out. Vidyavati's friendly welcome, Purna's almost casual helpfulness, my realization that two people were genuinely delighted at the success of a third, and a study group for newcomers led by a shy young man who introduced himself as Ratnaketu. The topic was 'leaving group values to become an individual'. This was good stuff. This was what I really wanted to be part of. I recently mentioned this study group to Ratnaketu and was surprised to find he had forgotten it; forgotten an incident so crucial in my spiritual life.

The alchemy somehow didn't work as well for Mary as it did for me, although she was happy enough with the evening. I remember saying to her in the car on the way home, 'That guy Ratna-whatever-his-name-was doesn't look as if he has been around all that long, but he's got some very good ideas. I think I'll come back.' Come back I did, and still do.

I report all this at some length in case you, the reader, are either thinking of seeking contact with Buddhists, or are a Buddhist who may be approached by a hesitant newcomer. To you, the hesitant one, I say, 'Go on. Do it. It's safe and friendly in there. There's nobody to be scared of but yourself.' And you, the Buddhist, never for a moment forget how important your first word on the phone or first handshake in the Centre could be to a fearful seeker. Just as mine did, a whole life, many lives, could depend on your initial expression of friendship. Don't just rely on your natural friendliness – it may need a real effort to break through the diffidence, shyness, even fear, of somebody whose need for the Buddha's teaching has driven them to seek you out.

Kawau cottage (c.1975)

*Small*,
my first effort at boat building (1961)

Old Bill with Ralph and me (1933)

Father (c.1935)

*Bucket* on a gentle day (1975)

The stupa at
Sudarshanaloka (1998)

The shrine at Kawau with
two gin bottles (1988)

Taranatha,
ordained this morning (15 June 1992)

Chetul Hut, Sudarshanaloka (1998)

# 17

# the discovery of compassion

Buddhism was slowly taking over my life. But it was hesitant and uncertain. Priyananda and Purna, the two members of the Western Buddhist Order I regarded as my teachers, were by now both in Britain, and my contact with teachers was tenuous. But the Buddha's teaching in its ways is 'wondrous strange', to quote a well-known Tibetan text.

What follows is a plain account of experience. It is of experience quite alien to my earlier life, and I suspect to the lives of many of my readers. The sudden appearance in consciousness of a strange archetypal figure was astonishing; the explosion of emotional energy from the unknown depths was overwhelming.

It is not appropriate at this point to enter a profound discussion on the Buddhist doctrine about the nature of Reality, but certain questions might be addressed. My conditioning, the common conditioning in the West, was towards the acceptance of waking experience, duly edited and rationalized, as reality. Other modes of experience, especially dream states, were seen as unreal, to be interpreted in terms of rational thought or entirely dismissed. The Buddhist tradition challenges both these assumptions. The world as we normally see it is not entirely real, neither is other experience entirely unreal. All experience is to be accepted as equally valid within its own context.

So it is with the events and experiences of meditation. These are not to be dismissed by the rational mind as fantasy, nor taken by the literal mind as fact. As with all other experience, they are symbolic approximations, approaches to a truth far beyond the reaches of the mundane mind.

In September, 1987, I joined the spring retreat at Kiwanis Camp, some thirty miles west of Auckland, on the narrow strip of land between the Waitakere Range and the Manukau Harbour. It was typical of many retreats that I attended over the years, a gathering of twenty to thirty assorted people of all ages, backgrounds, and experience, intent on meditating, studying Buddhism, and having fun away from home. But there was a potent, unpredictable alchemy pervading this particular meeting. The magic of the bush, the harbour, and the beach with its overhanging pohutukawas, the song of the tui and the multitude of other birds – and Prue. Prue was not long associated with Buddhism. Her spiritual interest was in yoga. Since there was a gap in the programme at 11 o'clock, Prue kindly offered to lead a session of yoga before the midday meditation. Before long, by popular request, she found herself leading yoga nidra, a guided visualization in which we were led through worlds of increasing beauty and magic. Conditions were ideal, and Prue's power far stronger than even she guessed. With several others I found myself overwhelmed, taken over by fantastic beauty, warmth, and love. Defences were dissolved away and the gates flung wide, giving onto deep, hitherto totally unknown recesses of my mind.

This experience was followed by the *metta bhavana* meditation practice, the development of universal loving kindness, of infinite goodwill to all beings. Beginning with meditation on acceptance and true love for myself, it expanded to encompass all beings in all places and at all times.* Having entered this practice in a glowing state of serenity – I had finished the yoga nidra that day sitting on a pale blue lotus in the middle of a serene lake contemplating my own image in a candle flame – I found myself in the last stage of the metta bhavana flying over Africa in a cloud of golden light. Below me were the starving thousands of Ethiopia. I was there among the sick and dying, my busy physician's hands working to relieve pain and suffering. There was a dark shadow above me. Looking down upon my proud, highly-trained hands from a harsh desert sky was a huge carved wooden mask, a dark, African face with an exaggerated mouth, a face of archetypal sorrow, reflecting the suffering of the world below. It was gone in a moment, but that moment was burnt indelibly into my memory.

Then came the voice from behind me, which I knew was the voice of Avalokitesvara, 'Those are not my hands!' Cold horror crept over me as I looked at my hands. They were indeed not his hands – there were no eyes in the palms!

As the vision faded I found myself sitting on my meditation stool aware of the bright sunshine, birdsong, the splash of ripples on the beach, and the prickling of cold sweat breaking out on my body.

---

* For further information about this and other meditation practices see Paramananda, *Change Your Mind*, Windhorse Publications, 1996.

I hardly knew Avalokitesvara at that stage of my life. In the Indo-Tibetan Buddhist tradition he is the embodiment of compassion, usually depicted with a thousand hands, each with an eye in the palm. I had glibly accepted him as my guide. I worked in a compassionate profession, helping the sick and suffering, so the connection was obvious. Why then the horror, the cold sweat of fear? As the hours passed the awful truth of the eyes in the palms began to penetrate. The eye of wisdom could see things as they really were; the hand, guided by insight, supplied what beings really needed, not just what I thought was good for them.

During the next few days the dreadful significance of the vision evolved, spurred on by the accusing voice, always from just behind me. 'Those are not my hands.' For almost thirty years I had been working to relieve suffering, guided, I had supposed, by compassion. But compassion arose not from self-centred pity, but from insight into the nature of self and other, without which true compassion – 'feeling with' – was not possible. Awareness and acceptance of myself was so rudimentary that I could not avoid seeing others largely as projections of my own needs. I was driven, at least in large part, to relieve my own pain, the pain that I felt on contemplating the pain of others. I had told myself that my hands were the hands of compassion. The awful truth was dawning – they were hands of pity, hands of power, even hands of greed.

After one particularly painful meditation I wandered the garden distraught and weeping, until I found myself back in the empty shrine-room seeking comfort from the figure of the Buddha on the shrine. But the room was not empty. Ratnaketu, still meditating in a shady corner, disturbed by my weeping, quietly escaped to report my state to Jayasri, the retreat leader. A few minutes later, as I sat in misery on the shrine-room steps, a gentle hand fell on my shoulder, with a cup of tea and an invitation to talk about it. Jayasri, bless her heart, responding with natural compassion to suffering. I talked as best I could through the convulsive sobbing. How much of it was intelligible I never enquired, but it served to clarify in my mind the dreadful lie that I had been living. But pride was not yet satisfied – there was still more work to be done.

'Those are not my hands!' As the days passed I sank further into self-pity and self-loathing. It was Friday morning. The retreat was to end on Sunday. I was to resume my role of family doctor, kind, wise, and compassionate, on Monday. I couldn't do it. I could not go back to what I now saw as hypocrisy.

I was walking into the front door of the old, white, weatherboard house on my way to the shrine-room for the morning meditation. Again the accusing voice, 'Those are not my hands!' Something finally rebelled. I would not be accused so! From deep inside me, angry and urgent, a silent voice screamed, 'Get off my back, you bastard! Most of the world thinks these hands are good enough.' Tears dribbled down my cheeks as I slumped on my meditation stool in misery, a hurt, resentful child, defeated and accepting defeat.

Through tight closed eyes I saw him, Avalokitesvara, gleaming white, no longer accusing me from behind but facing me, smiling gently, reaching with many hands to lift me into a self-accepting, upright posture of meditation. With each touch I felt his hands pouring love and acceptance into my body.

This time understanding was immediate. Compassion is not a commodity that I must dispense from my limited stock to the suffering. Compassion is a universal quality that pervades all. Compassion is for each and every being, including myself. Compassion is the ordinary response, to suffering, of a self-accepting, self-loving being wherever it manifests – including within myself. Compassion loves me too. If I lacked real compassion for others it was a measure of how little I loved and accepted myself.

Avalokitesvara had moved behind me and was chanting, not his own mantra, but '*sabbe satta sukhi hontu*' (may all beings be happy). My silent voice rose in joy from my heart to join the chant. Now the tears flowed freely – tears of joy and relief. I had broken through the prison wall. There was indeed a lifetime's work in developing insight and true compassion, but this first barrier of ignorance had been smashed.

The bell signalled the end of the meditation. The chant died away, the vision faded, and I found myself on my familiar stool, wet-faced, stuffy-nosed, and exhausted, but pervaded by a peace that I had never known. As I sat reflecting on the morning's events I was overcome by gratitude for Avalokitesvara's uncompromising love, a love with the courage to inflict pain if it must.

Saturday morning. I was still staggering from the beating I felt I had taken from Avalokitesvara's thousand hands. Since I was not the only one 'going through it' we had already decided not to continue the retreat programme on Sunday but to spend the day walking the ocean beach to assimilate our experiences and, where necessary, lick our wounds. How could I use the last two formal meditation sessions to consolidate the changes?

I sat limply on my stool. The time drifted past and nothing happened. 'If it all began in Ethiopia,' I thought, 'perhaps I should go back there.' As if it had been awaiting its cue, the mask reappeared, no longer a face of archetypal sorrow, but of ancient wisdom and love. From behind me came the familiar chant, 'sabbe satta sukhi hontu!' A pair of hands took me gently under the arms. I was carried high above the continent of Africa, flying south, then east, over the Indian Ocean, over Australia and the Tasman Sea, down the Rangitoto Channel and the approach to Auckland Harbour. Breathless with excitement I prepared to cross Auckland city and arrive back in the shrine-room; but nothing so predictable. A quick right turn opposite Castor Bay and I was suddenly being swished up my own front steps. I tried to greet my neighbour in her garden, but Avalokitesvara wouldn't wait. A bump, and I was sitting in the middle of my own living room. The experience is fixed indelibly in my mind, as real as any experience of my life. I was sitting on the floor looking over the channel to Rangitoto Island. Behind me Avalokitesvara's voice, now deep, full, almost triumphant, chanting 'sabbe satta sukhi hontu'. Rays of golden light pouring from his body to the ends of the universe. A ridiculous detail is stuck clearly in my mind: the light hitting the black flue of the space heater, which cast a shadow on the wall.

Again, the bell to mark the end of the practice, and for me the end of Avalokitesvara's teaching for that retreat. I have no memory of the remainder of that day, or even of coming back to my body in the shrine-room at the end of that practice. My next memory is the following morning, the last day before returning to 'normal' life in the city. The four of us who had shared our experiences during that week, Jayasri, Prue, Anne, and I, travelled the few kilometres to the coast in my car.

It was blowing a westerly, rolling the Tasman Sea onto Whatipu Beach in roaring walls of green and white. Chunks of white foam as big as my head were rolling up the beach, shattering themselves on whatever obstruction they met. Some very quiet people walked the beach, alone or in pairs, deep in reflection on their experiences of the past week, a word or a phrase shared over the roar of the sea from time to time. We were mostly content to be shielded from the need to speak by the noise. It was assimilation time, so necessary after a time of deep experience, but so often not allowed for in this world of constant hurry. As we drove back to the camp, four people still in thoughtful silence, Prue slipped a tape into the stereo – Allegri's *Miserere* sung by King's College Choir. It was too much for so soft a heart. Once more I was blinded by tears. Not wanting to switch the sublime voices off I stopped the car, and by common consent we sat in silence waiting for the tape to end.

The following day I went back to my practice as a family doctor. Everything was as I had left it. The book of appointments, with gaps for the inevitable emergencies. The stack of correspondence in the in-tray, all carefully sorted into business attended to by the secretary and neatly listed, matters needing my attention, the few personal letters that had found their way into my 'other world', and the list of junk mail that had already been consigned to the incinerator. My office, with my swivel chair partly hidden behind the corner of the desk, as it had been for the past twenty years. But there was something that was not quite right. Of course! There was no need to keep any barrier between me and the patient. To move the chair so that it stood clear of the desk was such a small change, but symbolically so important. I could still turn the chair on its swivel so I faced the patient obliquely if he or she seemed to be uncomfortable.

Somehow it no longer seemed necessary to shield myself in any of the traditional ways. My home phone number, for twenty-five years a closely-guarded secret, was now added to the letterhead, and in due course to the directory. 'Dr B.R. Hardwick-Smith, MB.; Ch.B.; D.C.H.; F.R.N.Z.C.G.P', proudly displayed on a black glass plate by the front door became 'Robin Hardwick-Smith, Family Doctor', a much more accurate description of who I now was. For the first time I was becoming fully protected from exploitation by the unscrupulous. Compassion called me to refuse to be taken in by unreasonable demands. Confidence allowed me, without a shadow of guilt, to tell a caller if I was unable to attend, and to send somebody else. My hours became better regulated. I even took time off for no better reason than tiredness. Before long the responses came, at first from elderly ladies, but in time from young and old. 'You are different – so much gentler – and you look so young and well!'

But the end of my medical career was in sight. Much as I enjoyed the new freedom of communication, the drive to serve people in the way I had been taught was running out. So much that I had been doing was losing its relevance. I began to see that what the people who came to me really needed could no longer be supplied through my old role as family doctor. The pursuit of understanding and compassion on a deeper level slowly began to take over my energy and time, until I found that I no longer looked forward with enthusiasm to my day in the consulting room.

People were still asking me for what society had trained them to ask: medicine in a biomedical form. There was plenty of scope for kindness, for sharing pain and grief, but the real need, the need for guidance towards spiritual growth and freedom, I was not yet qualified to meet, nor could I meet it from that role. Even healing, in the sense of interaction for mutual growth, was strictly limited by the expectations of scientific medicine.

Was the role of family doctor incompatible with the Dharma? It did indeed start to become so, not because a Dharmafarer couldn't practise good medicine, or because it called for the exercise of unskilful mental states, but because it demanded all my time and energy, and so did the Dharma. Eventually, three years after the Avalokitesvara retreat, I walked out of my office leaving the key inside, having sold my practice, and with it my right to practise family medicine in that district.

The silence in the deserted car park was deafening, and the freedom terrifying. It was a big, wide world out there, now that I no longer had my name plate and title to hide behind. My real life, for which I had been preparing for sixty years, was about to begin.

# 18

# opening the heart

However much of me the family doctor role had taken over, there were still parts that functioned outside it. By the time of the Avalo-kitesvara retreat I had left my wife of thirty years. Ysabel and I had never developed enough of a friendship to survive the departure of Liz, the last of our daughters to leave the family home, the previous year. For most of a year I had been living alone in a small house over-looking the Hauraki Gulf. It was a good period of my life, establishing myself as an independent individual after so many years of being hus-band and father. I was discovering deep joy in simple things: planning and preparing meals, arranging my home to suit my changing moods, listening to whatever music I chose whenever I chose, tending roses, and growing vegetables. Above all, I enjoyed the spur-of-the-moment invitations to friends to come round for a meal, or even stay for a night or two.

Life was stimulating and enjoyable, but it was far from idyllic. With the sudden increase in freedom came the need to deal with all sorts of neurotic attitudes and behaviours that had hitherto sheltered behind the restrictions of marriage and family. Not the least of these was a long suppressed craving for a loving sexual relationship. First as a glimmer, then as a glaring light, came awareness that I was lonely, that I had been lonely through years of a marriage lacking in intimacy, and that now I wanted warmth, intimacy, love.

It was into this setting that I returned from the dramatic up-heavals of the retreat to my much loved but solitary home. The follow-ing day, as I had done on several previous occasions, I called on Diane, manager of the Buddhist Centre bookshop, to return money and unsold books from the retreat. Diane, too, lived alone in a small house. She too that day was lonely, feeling the need for a fellow human being with whom to share experience. Responding to her receptive mood, I began telling her episodes from the retreat, then, tentatively, my own part in it, until I found myself revealing for the first time to another human being the profound experiences that had shaken me forever from complacency and ignorance. Diane responded with revelations of her own. So began one of the most important human relationships of my life.

We were a strange partnership – Diane living so much in her present experience as to be blown and buffeted by changing emotional states. I just beginning to emerge from a relatively conventional life, governed by thought and concept rather than by emotion and experience. Astonishingly, we communicated well enough to be able to grow together in the Dharma, to play together, and to develop what was for me the first mature friendship of my life. It was with Diane that I discovered new levels of emotional, physical, and spiritual intimacy for which my heart had been blindly groping for years. I even began to learn, hesitantly, fearfully, to be a little playful, to take risks, and to accept consequences that I could not anticipate. And it was with Diane that I discovered a gaping hole in my personality that I had somehow avoided seeing for so many years.

The love that Diane offered was rich and powerful, demanding a full-blooded response. To my horror, I found that the place from which that response was called was empty. Emotionally, even physically, I shrank from the passion of the embrace that part of me so longed for. Almost within my grasp had been the physical, emotional, and spiritual communion for which my heart had yearned. Now there was only baffled bewilderment and shame. At a stroke I had discovered a gross defect in my psyche, and a desperate need to overcome it. How fortunate I was to have developed a firm enough meditation practice to draw me back to my stool by the shrine. Scarcely knowing through my emotional turmoil what I was doing, or why, I sat myself before the Buddha image, surrounded by the familiar offerings of flowers, candles, and incense. I almost heard the legendary words of the Buddha-to-be as he took his place beneath the bodhi tree on the night of his Enlightenment, 'Though flesh may wither and blood run dry, I will remain here until I find the Truth.'

The events of that night were of a different order from the experiences of the Buddha, but for me almost as dramatic. From the image of pain and bewilderment in Diane's face as I had left her, emerged the defeated, agonized face of a trapped possum as I beat it on the head with an iron bar. I was back in my childhood garden, earning an honest wage in the manner approved by my society. Images of bloodshed and violence paraded through my tortured mind. Goats screamed and fell one by one as I applied my full concentration to the expert use of a precision instrument, the rifle that was a tool of my trade. A sheep thrown to the ground, head bent back round my left ankle, its blood gushing over my boot as the deftly wielded knife severed first the arteries, then the spinal cord. A squatting rabbit leaping high in the air, propelled by a bullet thudding into its warm body. On and on went the ghastly procession, until my suffering stirred life into the picture of Avalokitesvara in its oaken frame above the shrine. Choking with the horror of dreadful deeds, my shuddering body welcomed his hand reaching down my throat to drag from the depth of my heart great gouts of bloody shame and cast them out.

The image was gone. Limp, cold, wet with sweat, I slumped on my stool. So intense had been my revulsion that I found my shame had been physically vomited from me. But deep in my heart was a profound sense of relief. All that violence, committed in a state of wilful ignorance, had now been fully and horribly experienced. The deeds were now mine. I could accept responsibility for their consequences. I could begin to know that I was lovable. That gaping hole was closing.

Although this dramatic night was only a beginning of the healing – there have been many less traumatic encounters with past violence since then – the symptom of involuntary retreat from offered love never returned.

Not the least valuable product of this experience was the deepening of my understanding of karma. The Buddhist view of karma is essentially that every action or, more precisely, the state of mind behind every action, has an inescapable consequence. Actions arising from skilful states – i.e., generosity, love, and understanding – promote spiritual growth and happiness; actions arising from their opposites – greed, hatred, and delusion – inhibit growth or lead to regression to lower states of being. There is no suggestion of judgement, with its implication of an all-powerful judge meting out rewards and punishments. The results are an integral part of the actions. They just happen.

Until it emerged in response to Diane's love, I had been quite unaware that a fixed belief of being unlovable had been a guiding force in my life. In retrospect it is easy to see how this influenced the major choices in my life, especially the choice of the role of family doctor, with its repeated affirmation from twenty people asking me for help every day, and of marriage to a dependent, undemonstrative partner. Although my early environment of utility with denial of emotion undoubtedly set the stage, it was the history of violence that came tumbling out when I was driven to recognize the belief and seek its origin. If further proof of the connection were needed, it was right there in the loss of the symptom as soon as shame had been fully experienced. This was not the province of thought, concept, and speculation. This was naked experience, from which thought could naturally arise.

What next arose was the realization that violence and compassion are incompatible; they cannot coexist. The more violence I practised, the deeper I buried my capacity to love myself and others. Further, acts of gross violence that I performed almost daily for long periods of my life could only be carried out in states of deliberate suppression of awareness. Imaginative identification with other beings became too painful to live with. It, too, could only be locked away in hidden parts of the psyche. Out of sight is not out of mind, it is only out of control.

Awareness seems to be a global function. To suppress part of it is to dull all of it. Conversely, to awaken part of it carries the threat of awakening those parts that have been hidden ever since past events drove them underground. So it was with the awakening of my capacity to love and to be loved. So it has increasingly become since that time. Deliberately opening myself to the refining influence of beauty, especially the beauty of nature, awakens all aspects of sensitivity. Exposing myself to the joys and fears of intimate friendship allows the flowering of receptivity, responsiveness, and appreciation of self and other.

In the years that followed this awakening, more aspects of a long-buried acceptance of self appeared. It was Sunday evening at the end of a long, hard weekend of emergency medical duty. Diane had just arrived to watch a television programme with me. A few minutes before the end of my shift came a call to visit a man with abdominal pain. The lumps that filled his abdomen were obvious to the searching eye long before the examining hand confirmed their craggy nature. Nobody seemed to be aware that he was dying of cancer. Both patient and his family were talking about tests, to show what was wrong, then cure. I sat patiently with them, meeting their resistance and fear, denying my own exhaustion and increasing resentment against the family's doctor for what seemed to be heartless negligence in leaving them in such ignorance. Later, much later, collapsed in my favourite armchair, too exhausted and angry to sleep, I felt soft, loving fingers gently massaging my scalp. Suddenly, for the first time in memory, I knew that I needed nurture. I needed to be held, to be comforted, to be able totally to abandon responsibility for others, even for myself, and be a child. And I knew that that was OK. So came the learning that to ask for what one needs can be, and usually is, an act of kindness. To allow one's friend to give what she wants to give is simple generosity, which I had until now denied.

# 19

# alone

It was through relating to Diane that I discovered how much of my childhood I had buried. For most of my adult life I had related to others in the role of doctor or father. My adult response to other adults had been limited and superficial. People were met in their roles as colleagues or patients, as fellow golfers, fishermen, or squash players, as wife, mother, or children. Nowhere did I meet a human being, for only a self-aware person can meet another of its kind, and most of my self-awareness had been hidden in a back room from childhood.

But Diane was a woman, conscious, passionate, and demanding to be met. She was not passively acquiescing in the loss of her past as I was. She was going right in there to find it. If I wanted to relate to her, as I surely did, I would have to open doors to my own inner self. In particular, I was faced with finding my emotional energy, with knowing it at first-hand instead of meeting only the highly tamed and edited version that I had lived with to date.

By a strange coincidence, it was when these understandings were struggling to the surface that I happened on a set of taped lectures and exercises on raising self-esteem. They were in the most blatant 1970s Californian workshop style, but they had in them the guidance that both Diane and I needed at that moment. Surely another example of 'when the pupil is ready, the teacher will appear'. At any other time of my life I would have been so offended by the style that the content would not have reached me. Together we started work on this material. Or rather, each of us alone tackled what was relevant to us – much of it was highly sensitive, digging deep into the way we related to each other. But, by comparing experiences, we boosted each other's determination. I certainly would not have had the courage and persistence to do what I did on my own.

It was while this was going on that I faced up to my first solitary retreat. Twelve days alone at the Kawau cottage, facing myself for the first time without the protection of work, family, home, and garden. February 1988, the first week of the school year protecting me from interruption by the neighbours, all of whom had used their holiday time while the children were off school.

Some discoveries: Nakedness. Freedom from the symbolic restriction of clothing. Stepping from bed to walk into the dawn sea, and to wander, dripping salt water, in the bush, feeling at one with its sights, sounds, and smells. Meditating, studying, cooking, eating, swimming, walking, and sleeping, all in the freedom of nakedness.

Freedom from the tyranny of time. Taking off my watch was an even greater threat to my sense of propriety than taking off my trousers. Not to know the time of day was improper, a guilty liberty that would surely have its repercussions – but if it did, I don't remember them.

Fear. Bare, existential fear. It happened on the evening of the third day of solitude. Full moon on a summer sea. I stood on the jetty dripping sea water, lost in the wonder of the shimmering sea and the showers of phosphorescent sparks spraying from each drop that hit the surface. Behind me, the cottage – and fear. I could feel it growing, swelling like a mist from the sea, raising each hair of my neck into a tingling bristle, sending shivers up and down my back as it reached its frozen fingers to touch my shrinking, wet body. I had to move – I was cold and I hadn't so much as a towel to wrap about me. I had to face whatever it was that bred fear. As I turned towards the cottage I could see nothing different. The white shape of the cottage in the moonlight with a single, dim light in the window, partly hidden by the dark silhouette of the big gum tree. The boat-shed, white with its dark door, emerging from the shadow of the towering flame tree. But between me and the haven of the cottage was fear, a tangible, solid wall of fear. There was no escape, no other course to take but to walk into, and possibly right through, that terrifying barrier. The decision made and the body put in motion, the barrier seemed to change from a wall of fear to a physical obstruction through which I physically fought my way. It was like swimming through treacle. Each movement of each limb was a major effort, forcing against resistance as if held back by a thousand hands. In slow motion I reached for the door, pushed it open as if against a great resistance, lunged into the haven of the light, and latched the door behind me, leaving, so it seemed, the source of fear outside in the moonlight.

At no time during this experience did I suspect any objective source of fear. The fact that I knew it to be nothing but a projection of my own response to solitude did nothing to weaken its effect, or to slow my thumping heart. Fear had vanished, leaving me to contend with the symptoms of a massive dose of adrenaline. Within an hour, perhaps two, of sitting gazing on the supremely peaceful Buddha image on the shrine, the crashing heartbeat, tingling scalp, and prickling of sweat over my body, had given way to a sense of clarity, lightness, and strength that stayed with me most of the night.

Looking back on this experience from long afterwards, I have an image of defensive walls, normally held in place by the pressure of the outside world, falling away, as, for the first time in my life, the world was taken away. Being exposed to the world was not the problem. The world was not there. But for the first time I was experiencing being exposed to myself. The shock of losing my habitual defences, so familiar as to be unseen, was for a moment devastating. On the next two or three solitary retreats, always on the third day, a faint shadow of the old fear reappeared, and then it was gone. With it, incidentally, went other fears that I had lived with: the fear of sailing a small boat in a rough sea, the fear of riding a spirited horse, and even a large part of a major fear of heights.

Perhaps the biggest shock my value system suffered during those twelve days was from my indulging, sometimes for several hours a day, in seeking my personal needs through the self-esteem tapes. It was one tape, one short talk, with a set of exercises, that occupied much of that time. It was to do with meeting the younger self by a simple visualization practice. One was to imagine oneself walking in a country lane. In the distance is a tree, under which sits a child. As one approaches, one recognizes the child as oneself, at whatever age one chooses. The child recognizes the adult, and a conversation ensues.

At least, that was the theory. When I met my five-year-old he sat stony-faced and silent for several sessions. At last, when I could stand it no longer, I reached a cautious hand to his shoulder, at which he scuttled round to the other side of the tree to continue sitting in silent isolation. Cautiously following him, I ventured, 'You don't like me being here, do you?' to which he responded with a venomous, 'Fuck off!'

This was hardly encouraging, but not altogether surprising. He had, after all, been shut out of my life for over fifty years. If he was angry, fearful, and bitter when I had deserted him, how much more so would he be after all those years of rejection and denial. Even if he had wanted to greet me, to break through his isolation, he had no idea how to do it. But what shocked my adult self was not so much the hatred as the words he used to express it. I had not only denied the child for half a century, I had wiped the whole of his shepherd's culture from my memory.

Now I was on the defensive. I had made one mistake. Another could lose him completely.

'I just want to be your friend. Just sit with you for a while.'

Suddenly he turned towards me, fists raised. Two quick blows to my shoulder, a scream as from a terrified animal, and he was curled up on my knee, face pressed into my chest, sobbing, pouring out the misery of the years. I held him, at first fearful that he would break away and be lost for ever. As the storm settled, as his little body moulded more confidently into mine, I knew that we had found each other. So began one of the most important relationships of my life.

The child – neither of us ever found him a name – became a companion of my life, waking and sleeping, for some months, but it was in meditation that he really came alive. He had a habit of rushing in from my left as my concentration developed, his body hitting my thigh with a thump as his arms wrapped round my leg. Having made his ritual greeting he would slip his hand into mine, or take me firmly by the left thumb, and lead me into our day's adventures, sharing our lives as neither of us had ever done with anyone before. For me, the result was a surge of emotional energy that I had never experienced. Not only did I weep freely, mostly with joy, but to my astonishment I was able to enjoy the indulgence. I felt I was weeping all the tears that the child had never wept. For the child, it was life where there had been none before.

I had prepared myself for this exercise by bringing with me some childhood photographs. The child was partly modelled on one of them, a faded, hazy picture of my five-year-old self sitting with his back to an enormous bluegum tree. I found myself haunted by two more. One of myself aged about two, sitting on a pony with my two older brothers, and the other of an infant of about three months lying on a rug on a lawn. Now that I had the child's energy, I knew that I would be able to meet these long forgotten parts of myself. After the usual greeting one morning, taking the child's hand firmly in mine, I said, 'Come on. We're going to see the little guy.' He would have pulled away if my grip had been less determined. 'Aw, do we have to?' 'Yes. We need him as much as he needs us.'

As we approached the big, white gate leading to my childhood home, the old Box Brownie photograph materialized. Standing patiently beside the massive concrete post from which the gate hung open, was Sambo, the black Welsh pony, three boys huddled together on his back. The camera had caught for all time the unmistakable atmosphere of children posing under protest. But if the two older boys looked impatient to be about their business, the youngest, my two-year-old self, perched on the pommel of the saddle, was a picture of misery.

I lifted him from the pony and folded him in my arms, his passive body moulding like putty into mine. A gasp as he came to life, then a scream, and a series of almost mechanical wails from an expressionless face. What I held was a frozen bundle of fear, slowly becoming aware of itself. In time – was it minutes or hours? – as the little body thawed into responsive life, the screams died down into convulsive sobbing, and the child seemed to settle to sleep. I don't know where he went. I suspect that on finding warmth and peace he merely melted into my being. Whatever the explanation, I never met him again.

As if carried by a tide, the child and I were swept on, through the open gate, past the big bluegum beside whose gigantic trunk we had first met, drawn on by the picture of a baby, myself at three months, lying on a checked rug on the lawn. He looked so warm, alert, and lively, waiting to be picked up and cuddled. I reached for him, to find myself holding ... a wooden doll. The shocked silence was broken by a clear cry of anguish from the doll, 'Why do I have to suffer like this? I didn't ask to be born.' Then the horrified realization, 'But I did ask to be born. It was my choice.'

The tide would not wait. On and on I was carried, the child and the doll left somewhere in my wake. Suddenly there was no more movement, no feeling of being carried by some force towards some goal, only warmth, quiet, and peace. Totally supporting, enveloping peace. The relief at realizing that I was in the protection of the womb was momentary. Within me an urgent voice, 'I need to live. I need to get out of here and make my own decisions.' From even further back, 'Now that you have found the peace that you wanted, you don't like it. Don't ever forget this lesson!'

The decision made to live my own life – I have no doubt that it was a conscious choice – led me to a state of total chaos, that went on, it seemed, for ever. Total bodily disorientation, dazzling light, shattering noise, no reference point in time or space. (On reliving this experience the closest analogy I can find is of being rolled end over end in mountainous surf.) Then silence, stillness, and clarity. My awareness was contained in a tiny, infant body, black, shiny, and hard, lying on a hard, white surface. Was I minutes, hours, or weeks old? – I have no way of knowing. My mind was as clear and as hard as the obsidian body that held it. A clear, sharp thought arose, 'I won't be given the love that I need to survive, but I'm clever enough to get it for myself. I'll make myself a cheerful personality that people will notice and like.' The glass body was gone. I was back on my stool by the familiar shrine.

There would be little profit in trying to relate any of these experiences to history, even if that history could be known. But on the level of mythology, the meetings with my various 'younger selves' revealed several profound truths, which have made permanent changes in my life. The discovery that I was in some way responsible for my birth was not just an intellectual understanding. As a deep personal experience it was a truth beyond any threat from mere historical or metaphysical realities. The response of revulsion to the overprotection of the womb was another valid experience, carrying the message that there was no escape from dukkha, the unavoidable unsatisfactoriness of earthly experience, through regression or oblivion. Further, I now had direct experience via the obsidian infant of the origin of the cheerful, outgoing personality that had brought the attention I needed in childhood but had broken down as soon as I went to boarding school. Presumably the two-year-old on the pony was the reality behind the façade. He was certainly a preview of the fearful adolescent who emerged from that breakdown.

Had this been all that had happened during this, my first solitary retreat, I would have thought my time well used. But there was more to come. Towards the end of my twelve days, when I had gained enough confidence to wander far from home wearing only a straw hat and sometimes a tiny wraparound skirt, I found myself exploring a track I had not seen for years. As I rounded a sharp ridge, I found my way barred by a tall kanuka tree uprooted from the bank above by some storm and lying head down across the track. There was no way through the tangled branches, and below me was a precipitous slope with many loose rocks. The climb around the top was a bit daunting in the summer heat but, if I were to continue, it was the only way. Struggling up through roots and rubble, the midday sun scorching my bare back, I saw an elegantly shaped bottle projecting from under a root. With a little gently wobbling it came free, to expose another buried beneath it, and the shattered remnants of several more. They were indeed prize specimens, Old Pensioner gin bottles, with the motif of a Chelsea Pensioner outlined in low relief on the flat side. They had probably been some long forgotten alcoholic's emergency store. Both had rusty caps in place, and seemed to be full of water. For ease of carrying I punctured the caps with a stick and poured the water onto the hot, parched clay, splashing my legs generously in the process.

The smell of gin billowing up from the hot ground washed over me, bringing to my solitude-sensitized mind jumbled memories of years of savouring gin, at home, at sports clubs, in boats, on beaches, in bars, and in the very cottage that was my refuge for this retreat. Back to my lips and tongue came the craving that I thought had died ten years before, and with it a sick fear of again falling into the slavery of alcoholism. Clutching the empty bottles I ran down the long, dusty track, past the cottage, and straight into the cleansing sea, there to reflect on the vulnerability that the old familiar smell had awakened. Until this demon was exorcised I could not rest. First I filled the bottles with clear rainwater, then arranged within them the finest floral displays I could create, to place on either side of the Buddha on the shrine. A short period of meditation to settle my determination before the long, hot climb back to the fallen tree. I could not rest easy until I was quite sure there were no more full bottles hiding in the rubble.

I wonder what a passing traveller would have thought, had I been seen, naked but for a hat, furiously digging with a garden fork among the tangled roots, yellow dust caking my sweat-covered body. Nothing more turned up but broken glass and the lingering smell of gin. Satisfied at last, I walked wearily back to the healing sea to wash away the fearful memories.

# 20

# testing the water

1989 could have been an idyllic year. I was well established in my little house at Castor Bay. The roses responded, as roses will, to every touch of loving care with extravagant displays of blooms – red, white, yellow, and even blue, many of them with a fragrance that permeated the still evenings. The view over the familiar gulf, ever changing, ever interesting, was a constant companion. For most of my time at home I enjoyed solitude, a much needed antidote to thirty years of family life, but I also had the freedom to invite friends for a meal, a study group, or a casual chat. With Diane I shared meditation and the Buddhist path, as well as warmth, intimacy, and deepening friendship.

My medical practice, too, was maturing. Not without prolonged soul-searching, I passed the night and weekend emergency work to younger colleagues. My professional life moved with a slower and steadier rhythm. I gave more time to those things I found especially interesting – minor surgery, counselling, and problems of alcohol and drug dependence.

But I was in my sixtieth year. If I were ever to take my spiritual practice seriously, and make the changes that becoming a follower of the Buddha called for, I was fast running out of time. I had already absorbed enough of the teaching to recognize the 'god realm' that I was sinking into – that dangerous state of pleasure and comfort that leads to complacency, then apathy and stagnation. I had seen too many people die wondering what their lives had been for, to relish that prospect.

So the decision was made, not to renounce all worldly ties immediately and meditate in a mountain cave, but to go to Britain for three months to discover what the Buddhist life, at least life in this particular Buddhist movement, was all about.

Thirty-four years previously, a brash 25-year-old had spent five weeks at sea heading towards an unknown professional future. Now a man approaching old age spent twenty-seven hours flying towards an equally unknown spiritual future. Echoing in my ears were words from Lama Govinda's classic, *The Way of the White Clouds*:

Just as a white summer-cloud, in harmony with heaven and earth, freely floats in the blue sky from horizon to horizon, following the breath of the atmosphere – in the same way the pilgrim abandons himself to the breath of the greater life that wells up from the depth of his being and leads him beyond the farthest horizons to an aim that is already present within him, though yet hidden from his sight.

Was I just such a pilgrim, tuning in to those forces that would carry me to spiritual heights, even to Enlightenment itself? The events of the next few weeks were to show that I was not – at least not yet. Suddenly bursting into tears on a train, while reading those words of Lama Govinda, broke the news to me. I was homesick, yearning for Diane, home, and family. It was going to be a long journey. Fortunately, it was to be some years before I discovered how long.

During those critical months I attended meditation retreats at Vajraloka, the movement's meditation centre in North Wales, and study retreats at Padmaloka, the training centre for men aspiring to join the Western Buddhist Order, in the Norfolk countryside. Even at this early stage of my spiritual journey, strange things were happening. One day as I sat on my stool in the old barn at Padmaloka, I heard a voice, strangely like my own but coming from the back of my head. 'You stupid old goat, sitting there trying to be the Buddha. You'll never do yourself or the world any good like that. Why don't you go home and grow carrots? You do that well!'

The voice of soul-destroying doubt. That refusal to make the unconditional commitment without which no real change can happen. Holding back the tears I walked to the nearby marshes where there was a hide for bird watchers. Safely protected from the accusing world that knew that the goal I was striving for was hopeless, I let the flood of self-pity flow until, some hours later, exhausted, hungry, and thirsty, I began to come to my senses. It was indeed a daunting task I was undertaking. And I was certainly heading into my declining years. But I had no option. There was nothing left in my life that was worth doing except what Buddhists call going for refuge to the Three Jewels, deepening my commitment to the ideals of Enlightenment, the way to Enlightenment, and the fellowship of all who follow that way. Expanding my awareness and compassion until my life was guided by unlimited wisdom and love for all beings. Doubt had not given up the struggle. It took several more trips to the haven of the birdwatchers' hide during the next few days to shed more tears and to strengthen my resolve before I could unreservedly face my future. But, like Kipling's 'Cat That Walked By Itself', I didn't tell anybody.

One day I paid a formal visit to Sangharakshita, the English monk who founded the Western Buddhist Order. Sangharakshita, the spiritual, intellectual, and literary giant whose writings and taped lectures I had studied, discussed, and admired for the previous five years, turned out to be a smallish, slightly untidy, friendly English gentleman, just a few years older than myself. Perhaps I could detect signs of his genius – perhaps I was merely trying to sustain the romantic image I had built up. It has taken me several meetings over some years to reconcile these two aspects of this remarkable man. But the conclusion I am forced to accept is that, having lived most of his life on a level of awareness beyond my imagination, he must remain to me, and most on my level, an enigma. I also had the good fortune on my last day in England to meet Subhuti, one of Sangharakshita's earliest disciples, who was later to become my principal teacher and preceptor.

I had come to Britain with a question. Did I want to change my way of life, to leave home, family, and Diane to move to Britain and train for ordination into the Western Buddhist Order? Did I want to move away from my profession and social position towards simplicity, relative poverty, and a life based on spiritual endeavour and service? By the time the Piccadilly Line train had decanted me at Heathrow Airport to begin my return journey, the answer was clear. Yes, I did want to make these changes.

It was not that I was unhappy with my life's achievements to date. I had certainly made a poor showing as a husband and father, but the best thing to do about that was to become a better person, and hopefully repair some of the damage. All things considered, it could have been worse. At least I had stuck to my responsibilities until my presence was no longer necessary.

My career as a family doctor had fared much better. I had given good service to very many people, who received me as a respected guest in their homes. I had been closely involved with teaching and administration in my academic college, which had granted me an honorary Fellowship. The alcohol problem had been a close call, but now, fifteen years later, I was confident that that demon had been subdued. I was not leaving my old life because I had made a mess of it. I was leaving it because it was limited, confined to the practical, material sphere of experience, and that was not enough. Had I been able to expand into the spiritual sphere at a much earlier age, I could possibly have developed all aspects of my life together. Now it was clearly either/or. One department had had its turn, now it was time for the other.

Such were my thoughts as I settled into my seat for the 27-hour return journey. The roar of turbojets, the familiar pressure of the accelerating seat on my back, and Britain, together with my new-found teachers and support systems, receded into the distance.

Back at Castor Bay, and the office in which I had worked for nearly half my life, the options didn't look quite as clear. I would certainly have to return to Britain, but first I had, gently, to withdraw from the medical practice, starting by reducing to three days a week, putting a bit more effort into Buddhist studies and activities, and not being too dramatic about changes in case I had reactions.

I drifted along for nine months, until an opportunity arose to sell the practice. By this time I had put a great deal of effort into antici-pating retirement, discovering and acknowledging grief, and loosen-ing my attachment to my professional role. So it came about that, having left my professional persona fixed to the office door, stripped of my familiar armour, I became just a man called Robin. In spite of all my preparations it was an unknown and fearful world that I faced.

# 21

# the family within

By the time my summer solitary retreat came round, I was almost expecting the incredible to happen yet again. But the start of this retreat was prosaic enough. I was back in the familiar surroundings of Kawau. The school holidays were over, and the other families from the bay were safely back in the city. Sun, the whisper of ripples on the beach, the ever-present voices of tuis and chaffinches, and the lazy whirr of cicadas. Rolling from bed in the dawn to walk the few steps to the sea, then to walk naked and dripping in the magically beautiful valley behind the house, until I had located enough awareness of my body to be able to begin the mindfulness of breathing meditation by my shrine. This shrine, built lovingly in the first day or two of the retreat, of course featured Avalokitesvara, his white figure presiding over a slab of sandstone covered with white silk and liberally decorated with white lilies, with which the valley abounded. Later in the day, a period of study. This time it was Sangharakshita's commentary on the *Vimalakirti Nirdesa*. Then metta bhavana, walking, more swimming, a meal, and sleep.

Probably that is all that would have happened had somebody not left in the house a copy of *What We May Be*, a treatise on psychosynthesis by Ferrucci, a pupil of Assagioli, who had founded this particular school. Idly opening this book one afternoon, I found myself reading about sub-personalities. As I remember it, what the author was saying was that if we allowed our various partly-conscious emotional tendencies to be embodied, to become personified, then we could interact with them, and they with each other, in our imagination. So we could come to know our own tendencies, bring them into full consciousness, and allow them to overcome their differences and work together in harmony.

This seemed a great idea. So much better than the ghastly and fruitless psychoanalysis I had undergone twenty-five years earlier when I had first tried to face alcoholism. It could be fun, and since I could try it by myself, and give up if it didn't work, why not?

That afternoon's meditation was approached with mixed feelings. 'Bound to be an anticlimax,' I firmly told myself as I settled my naked body on my stool. These sub-personalities must be elusive or they would not have been in hiding all these years. No hurry. Wait until the mental chatter settles and I slip into the relatively calm, clear state of access concentration. Then invite them in.

The effort to calm the mind suddenly seemed less. There was a quiet exhilaration as awareness of the surging tide of the breath displaced all thoughts, plans, even sexual fantasies, from my mind. Access concentration. And with it the courage to ask, 'Who's been driving me all these years?' Suddenly, as if he had been awaiting this moment for a long time, he appeared. This man, I knew, was one of the most important people in my life. He was rugged, tough, about thirty, of medium build, but in every sense strong and determined, a man to get things done. He wore jeans and a denim jacket, working boots, and a miner's cap complete with lamp. I already knew him, but courtesy made me ask, 'Who are you?'

'I'm the guy that gets things done around here. I have responsibilities. A family that depends on me, kids to feed, people to be looked after. Somebody has to attend to all the things that need to be done, and that somebody is me. I don't have time to be swanning around sitting on cushions trying to be the Buddha. I have to get on with it.'

His voice was becoming harder and angrier.

'I haven't got time to be hanging round talking to dozy bastards that don't give a damn about who needs things done. And now get to hell out of my way or I'll kick you in the guts!'

Even he seemed shocked by the anger that was welling up. In my sensitive meditative state I was horrified. My awareness snapped back to the room, the pressure of the stool on my buttocks, the breeze from the window, and the prickle of cold sweat over my body. But the vision of the man – and his anger – remained.

This was the man whose highest purpose was to provide for his tribe. He and the world supposed he did this in love, that his lack of concern for his own needs and devotion to the needs of his family arose from compassion. His face and voice were those of my older brother, Ralph, but his driving purpose was that of my father. The anger? Well, that was doubtless my father too, although I rarely saw a sign of it, and, I suspect, even more rarely did he. His name was Provider. How thin the veneer of compassion hiding his real driving motives, anger and guilt, we both discovered within minutes of our first conscious meeting. Here indeed was a man I needed to know and work with. Surprisingly, I scarcely gave the miner's cap any thought. It was some days before I discovered its significance.

Somewhat chastened by this experience, I approached meditation a little obliquely the following afternoon. This time the question was a bit more cautious. 'Is there somebody there who loves and laughs and enjoys?' And there she was, much the same age as Provider, but different in every other detail. A woman, podgy, pale, and tender, wearing a shapeless smoky-blue skirt and jacket. But far from laughing, she was weeping streams of tears that dribbled down her cheeks and splashed on her bulging jacket. This time the question was genuine. 'Who are you?'

'I am your awareness of emotion. I weep Avalokitesvara's tears for the suffering of the world; I weep tears of joy for the beauty of a sunset, a birdsong, a symphony. I weep all the tears that I never wept in childhood. I'm soft, loving, responsive, and I'm becoming so much more aware of all the things I weep for: beauty, love, sadness, grief, you, me.'

As she spoke, her podgy hands fluttered about, ever returning to press into her heart. She was totally taken over by each and every experience and emotion. Even at this first meeting it was clear that most of her tears were of joy, the joy of discovering that she was alive.

Reflection on the blue woman came up only with her name, Fountain (could she be anybody else with her constant weeping?), and the realization that I needed to work with her every bit as much as I did with Provider.

Over the next few days four more sub-personalities emerged, complete even to their names, from the depths of my meditating mind. First, the Urchin, a boy of about eight or nine, a shock of hair standing straight up, freckles, cheeky grin, torn shirt, shorts, and bare feet. I knew him well. He was the childish energy, enthusiasm, and playfulness I could never remember. He was irresponsible, irrepressible, selfish, childish fun. I was to discover before long that he was also a survivor, streetwise and cunning. Next to appear was a small, wiry man wearing shorts and elastic-sided boots, a hand-rolled cigarette stuck to his bottom lip. His legs were slightly bowed, and he walked with his left shoulder thrust forward, as if he were edging round an obstacle. His name, I discovered at that first meeting, was not Busy-Fix-It, as I had suggested, but *Mister* Busy-Fix-It. And Mister Busy-Fix-It he remained for some years, until with the mellowing of age he consented to drop the title. Following him was the organizer in my life who appeared as the General, and after him a sad, needy youth who insisted that his name was Cur.

Now that I had assembled my team, what was I to do with them? Or, rather, what would they do with themselves? More importantly, who *were* they? Obviously they were much more than mere embodiments of my subconscious traits, although that is where they seemed to have come from. These were individuals with fully formed personalities, with their own likes and dislikes, joys, and sorrows. 'Allow them to interact with one another, and with yourself' was fine, but did they want to? Before I went much further, there was an intriguing statement in Ferrucci's book that needed investigation. The gist of it was that the sub-personalities, as well as personifying subconscious tendencies, were degraded forms of one's personal archetypes, an archetype, in this sense, being an embodiment of a universal principle such as wisdom, compassion, and energy. He suggested a technique for inducing them to revert to their archetypal forms which was delightfully simple. Merely take a walk with the sub-personality up the Mythical Mountain, whose summit overlooks the universe, and if he or she wants to, the transformation will happen. Now this was no light-hearted affair. One does not take a trip up a mythical mountain with a passing acquaintance. This would call for cooperation and trust. In fact it would seem to be a big test of commitment for both parties.

The first volunteer for the assault on the Mythical Mountain was Provider. In my meditation arose an image of a region I knew from my many walks, a track leading through a densely forested valley to a rocky peak rising high above the surrounding broken hills. As we set off up the valley Provider strode on ahead, head thrust forward and hands deep in pockets. I reminded him he had given me half a day to walk with me, not away from me. His walk slowed, and he allowed himself to become more interested in his surroundings. With each step he became more friendly and helpful. As we climbed on, his appearance began to change, his body becoming almost radiant, glowing with a mysterious light from within.

Emerging from the forest onto the moss-covered peak of the mountain, Provider stood, arms upraised, looking over the universe. A voice from far away. 'I begin to understand all about providing. I see all beings from here for ever – I know them – I love them – I provide in love and joy. I am Avalokitesvara!' The image faded. I was back on my stool in the little cottage on the edge of the bush, weeping in pure joy and wonder.

Except for Urchin, who couldn't be diverted from making a dam in the stream, each of the others in turn made the climb with me, but returned, perhaps a little more aware but essentially unchanged, until I finally found the courage to invite Fountain. For reasons I did not understand, I had been reluctant to ask her to climb the mountain. It was not just that she was bulky, soft, and not very fit. There was an intensity in her experience that seemed both fragile and foreign. This was strange territory that I was hesitant to enter. But the choice was not mine. No sooner had I brought her to mind than she was with me, intensely involved in everything about us.

After the familiar climb, up which Fountain seemed to float rather than walk, we came at last to the summit and stood gazing out over the universe. Fountain stood, bulky and smoky blue:

'I feel the joy and pain of all beings. I share their anger, fear, guilt, and love. I feel the beauty of the world and each tiny part of it....'

As she spoke, her figure was becoming indistinct, translucent. Within the blue, soft, hazy exterior there appeared another figure. It was a slim, athletic young woman in close-fitting emerald green, which covered all but her hands, feet, and face. Her short fair hair was covered with a matching green cap. Through a hazy blue aura, her figure glowed with the familiar sourceless light. The voice, now that of the radiant, young woman, continued, 'I feel the joy and suffering of each individual far, far more than they can.'

There was a pause, a hesitation, as if she were searching her experience, then, as from far away, 'My name is Tara!'

This goddess was nothing like gleaming white Tara whose picture I remembered from some far time and place; nothing remotely like any ordinary memory. But that she was real, and that she embodied unimaginable compassion, I had no doubt. She stood, silently absorbing her new understanding, while I, totally overwhelmed, became enveloped in the blue aura. So I stood with her for a time, but time and place were no longer relevant. This was, in fact, my first remote glimpse of eternity – experience beyond time-space. The image faded, and I was back on my stool in front of the shrine, all alone in the little cottage by the beach.

There was a strange discontent. Now that I had met Avalokitesvara and Tara, my world could never be the same. But they were up there on the top of the Mythical Mountain and I was down here in

the valley. There was a limit to how helpful even these glorious archetypal beings could be if they stayed up there. The book said nothing
about bringing them home. In fact I had a private feeling that the
beings I had met were way beyond what Ferrucci had in mind. So I was
on my own with my growing determination not to lose these experiences. I could not imagine myself living up there on the mountain; I
would just have to try to bring them down onto my level of
experience.

Back to the meditation stool, to the familiar process of allowing
my mind to become still, absorbed in the tide of the breath. To my
delight, there stood Avalokitesvara, just as I had left him. Again I was
absorbed in his form, as his (our) silent voice continued, 'I see all
beings and their suffering. I provide in love and joy to lead them to
freedom. The more I can give, the more is my joy, limited only by their
capacity to accept freedom.'

Slowly 'we' began to follow the path into the bush and down
the mountain. No sooner were we in the shelter of the trees than the
towering figure began to shrink and I felt myself becoming separate.
By the time we reached the lookout, Avalokitesvara had reverted to
the old figure of Provider, complete with cap.

'All those people in the valley,' I asked him. 'Do you still see
them in love and compassion?'

'It's too big for me. They can look after themselves. I have my
own responsibilities.'

As we approached the valley floor, Provider's step became more
determined. 'It's a lot of bloody nonsense caring for the whole world.
I'm pretty capable, but I've got my work cut out caring for my own
family. If I took on even the family next door I would make a balls-up
of the whole thing. No, I'm going to look after my own lot and do it
properly.'

He sat on a log, isolated, head bowed with the load of his anger.

'You poor, angry man,' I told him. 'Look up to the top of the
mountain. You know what's there. You don't have to bind yourself in
all this anger.'

He looked up, weeping openly for the first time in his life, as I
wept with him, he in anger and I in grief for a life spent with love shut
out. As we clung together, pent-up love and anger poured out, mixing
in whirlpools of unconfined energy.

All this was a bit discouraging. I had surely discovered a lot
about Provider, but my acquaintance with Avalokitesvara was

tantalisingly brief. He had made it plain that we lived on different levels, and that if I wanted to be with him it would have to be in his world. However, there was still Tara. By now I had done some research into her identity. I found that, according to Indo-Tibetan Buddhist legend, she had emerged from a lotus floating on a lake of tears shed by Avalokitesvara in response to the suffering of the world. Her special function was to carry transcendental compassion from the highest heavens down to earth, where it was most needed. Perhaps she would come home with me.

Once more to the shrine to mount the wooden stool which by now was becoming a chariot to mythical worlds. As the meditation deepened I found myself emerging from the bush into a clearing at the top of the mountain. There she stood, slim, radiant, and so beautiful in her vitality that I could only weep tears of joy in her presence. I could feel the aura of her profound perception of the joy and suffering of all beings. I had not realized until that moment that perception of suffering also meant perception of joy. After standing long in silence, 'I am ready to go down now.'

I still hear that voice as I heard it then, clear as a mountain stream, strong, confident, the voice of a goddess, yet of a woman and a friend. As she walked towards the bush track, her movement was graceful beyond my imagination. For a moment I wondered if she was floating, but her bare feet were certainly touching the ground, the tussocks bending – or was it bowing? – beneath her feet.

As we moved onto the valley floor she spoke again. 'People won't be able to see me as I am. If they see me at all it will be as Fountain, a bit podgy, soft, kind, loving, and blue. You and some others will sometimes see me clearly, sometimes not.' Then she was gone.

For the next few months one, other, or several of these subpersonalities would appear spontaneously during meditation. As their individual qualities gradually became more integrated into my personality, most of them began to fade. But not Tara – who developed, and is in fact still developing, as the embodiment of my spiritual aspiration – or Provider, who for many years has represented my more earth-bound activity. A quote from a diary written only a few days after I first met Provider:

> Provider still sits on his log where I left him a few days ago. He takes off his miner's cap and puts it on the log. 'I don't think I'm going to need that any more.'

I ask, 'Why do you wear it?'

He smiles crookedly. 'It's hard under the cloth. Protection. You could say it's my hard headedness. Ha, ha! You see, it's got a light that points straight ahead. Keeps me on course so I don't get distracted... Doesn't seem relevant any more.'

Then, with a touch of his old, consuming anger, 'I feel like a bloody steer. No balls any more.'

And another, written two years later towards the end of six months of end-to-end retreats in Britain and Spain:

On a scorching hot mountainside one afternoon I suddenly felt disgusted with the lifestyle I had adopted. Six months of indulging in my own whims. Nothing useful done for anybody. This was old stuff, so familiar that I was not surprised to see Provider sitting beside me:

'I've always worked for the good of the tribe – always had to. Now you are telling me I don't have to. Do you want me to lie down and bloody die? You don't know what you ask. You tell me to do what I enjoy. That means accepting that I have needs. Well that just isn't me. Personal feelings and needs just aren't me.'

This was a big one. The retreat was being led by Surata, a man of wisdom and eloquence. Perhaps he could help. So I explained to Surata that Provider was out of a job, and was so unhappy that he was causing trouble. 'What do you mean, out of a job? He's got the whole universe to provide for!' Later that same evening, Provider's thoughtful voice slipped into my meditation.

I thought I provided in love. Now I know I provided in anger and guilt, yes, and fear too. I can't provide for the universe that way. It will mean retraining.... But the job is me.... It certainly is me.... OK, I'm on!

One question remains. Who are these sub-personalities? What is their status in the order of things? Tara is of a different order, but who are all the others? It would be easy to dismiss them as creations of a fertile imagination, which in one sense they undoubtedly are. On the next level of reality they could be seen as subconscious tendencies – what

Buddhists call *samskaras* – embodied and given independent form. Again, there must be an element of truth, but here the intriguing thing is, how is their form determined? Provider's cap with its complex symbolism was certainly no deliberate concoction of my conscious mind. When I first met it I had no idea of its meaning. Other symbols remain unexplained. Why was Fountain so uncompromisingly blue? What was the significance of Busy-Fix-It's elastic-sided boots? Yet all these symbols were present, fully developed, at first meeting.

The nearest comparable experience I can think of is dream symbols. The sub-personalities had many of the qualities of the dramatis personae of dreams, whose complex symbolism frequently amazes me. Dream symbols, too, will, in my experience, act out their messages if suitably invited, although I have never met one who acted so convincingly and over such a long period. So my conclusion is that this whole exercise was similar to a protracted lucid dream (a dream in which the dreamer is aware that they are dreaming and is able to some extent to guide the dream's progress). Whatever the truth of the matter, the experience has been an enormous help to the process of integrating my scattered pieces into a semblance of a human individual.

# 22

# subhuti and friendship

If there was any possibility of my slipping back into the god realm, the state of undiluted pleasure depicted in the Tibetan Wheel of Life, which leads to apathy and stagnation, it would not be for long. Four months after I stepped out of my family doctor role, Subhuti arrived in New Zealand to lead a study retreat for men who had asked for ordination within the Western Buddhist Order.

To those who hadn't met him, Subhuti was a man full of surprises. The son of a naval officer and product of public school and university, he had arrived in Sangharakshita's nascent Buddhist movement via the late hippie culture. Never one to waste time, he was ordained with minimal preparation, as were all members of the very young Order. Responsibilities crowded round him like bees to a honeypot, which brought to light his special quality of leadership. Subhuti leads from the front. Teams form behind him, and major things are achieved. One of the more spectacular exploits of his early career was, while not being quite sure which end of a hammer did what, and with no visible means of financial support, undertaking to convert a burnt-out East London fire station into a Buddhist centre and residential accommodation for up to twenty people. Such was his naive faith and energy that from those scorched bricks rose the London Buddhist Centre, still one of the largest and most active centres in the movement.

Subhuti came almost directly from leading an ordination retreat, during which he not only joined the ordinands in shaving his scalp, but had the misfortune to lose a crown from an upper incisor. Gap-toothed, his cherubic face surmounted by a surprised-looking stubble, he faced his audience on the first night of the retreat with the announcement that he was going to talk about going forth – leaving behind all that inhibits one's spiritual growth, symbolized by the Buddha-to-be leaving his home and family to become a wandering ascetic – and going for refuge to the Three Jewels (commitment to the ideals of the Buddha, his teaching, and the fellowship of all who follow that way).

I was not impressed. As Subhuti began, rather hesitantly at first, to speak, I was silently muttering, 'We didn't bring you half way round the world to tell us all this old stuff. Surely you can do better than this.' An hour later I was sitting in stunned silence. What I had heard was nothing I hadn't heard before, but this time the message had side-stepped all defences to score between the posts. I could never be the same again. The message was simple. One can go for refuge only as fully as one has gone forth. One can commit oneself to one's ideals only as fully as one has put aside previous attitudes and behaviours that are inconsistent with those ideals.

Going forth from my role of family doctor had been a major undertaking, calling for long preparation and such symbolic acts as cancelling my medical registration and resigning from the College of General Practitioners, which had recently elected me as a Fellow. Breaking free from attachment to partner, family, house with its roses and sea view, car, television – all those people and objects that contributed to my identity – was a daunting prospect indeed. Contemplating an assault on the habitual views of who I was – 'I am this sort of person, not that sort of person' – so strongly linked with my lifestyle of sixty years, was overwhelming. But, as Subhuti had so eloquently stated, there was no spiritual progress without renunciation, no going for refuge without going forth, no rebirth without previous death. If I wanted more from the rest of my life than the futile exercise of distracting myself from the knowledge of impending death, and I most surely did, then I would have to leave Castor Bay, leave New Zealand, soon, and possibly for ever.

Over the next ten days, Subhuti gave a series of talks and led study on spiritual friendship. My arrogance had been dealt a shattering blow. With growing humility I listened, reflected, and joined in the discussion.

Spiritual friendship, held in high esteem by the Buddha, is encouraged in the FWBO as an important spiritual practice. This is not the most appropriate place to set out to discuss a practice that has ramifications into the furthest corners of the Dharma. However, the more mundane aspects of friendship, the free association of individuals for their mutual benefit, were very much the stuff of this phase of my growth.

I was not the only one present who felt a bit awkward about making a study of friendship. Wasn't friendship a magical thing that happened by some sort of alchemy, like falling in love? Wasn't it a bit indecent, even blasphemous, to investigate it as one might the bio-chemistry of gastric secretion? Subhuti obviously didn't think so.

During the first few days I discovered a great deal about the nature of friendship in general, and the lack of it in my life in particular. When discussion moved on to how to change all that, things became really interesting. 'If you want a friend,' Subhuti said firmly, 'don't hang about – go and make one.' This, I thought, is too much. Life is not like that. But from subsequent discussion, and experience over the following years, I found that life *is* like that. Actively going out to a potential friend, deliberately working on discovering who they are, on meeting difficulties and developing common interests, can be a very rewarding practice indeed. The best friendships I have ever known have arisen this way. Of course there are many other factors. The potential of a friendship depends on the importance of shared interests. Nowadays, all my friends share an interest in spiritual development, which sets the potential limits of friendship almost at infinity.

Again, I must thank my friendship with Diane for opening my heart and mind to the intimacy without which no friendship can go far. For me, as for so many men in my society, intimacy was a danger-ous thing, to be approached cautiously, and only in the context of a sexual relationship. Intimate friendship with another man was highly suspect. It was in the relationship with Diane that I first began to over-come that fear of intimacy. Without that experience, the deep friend-ships I have subsequently developed with other men would probably never have started.

But for all the joy and learning that can come from a friendship based on a sexual relationship, there is a catch. Sex involves an irre-ducible element of self-centred desire, which limits the depth that friendship can attain. Ultimately, the stuff of friendship is transcend-ence of self-interest in the unlimited communication between two individuals. So, although friendship within a sexual relationship may be the deepest, possibly the only, friendship available to many people, friendship uncomplicated by sexual desire can go a long way further. This is now so much a part of my experience that I marvel at the resistance I then had to accepting it. I even engaged in a heated argument with Subhuti – heated, that is, on my part – until, with his usual kindness and humour, he suggested for my consideration that the energy I was giving to the argument could indicate that it con-tained more emotion than reason. There was no answer to that – it was transparently true. Yet another of life's lessons learned. The stronger our emotional attachment to an argument, and the more vehemently we defend it, the less reason there is likely to be behind it, and the more likely it is that we are defending a position rather than seeking the truth.

# 23

# going forth

With first the Avalokitesvara retreat of two years previously, then the sobering revelations arising from Subhuti's talks, the complacency of my self-view was shattered. I could not contemplate going back to my old ways, nor could I remain among the broken views scattered about me. There was no alternative. I had to go forth. Fortunately for me, two other men on that momentous retreat had reached the same conclusion. The fact that they were both much the same age as my older children seemed irrelevant. We planned to shoulder our packs and set off together for Britain to do whatever was necessary to gain admittance to the Western Buddhist Order and a life of service to the spiritual needs of all beings.

In the event, Mark and Richard set off without me. A familiar bellyache that suddenly exploded into biliary colic called for surgery before I could safely travel to distant lands. As the day of the operation approached, my lifelong heartburn began etching a plan in my mind. While the surgeon is working in my upper belly, I thought, why doesn't he fix the hiatus hernia too, and relieve me of that nuisance? When I put this idea to him it was met with acquiescence, but did I detect a trace of reluctance? As it turned out, it was not a very good idea. The relief, although dramatic, faded after a year or two. Much worse was the prolonged convalescence and later development of multiple incisional hernias requiring more surgery a few years later, all of which arose from the need for an upper midline incision to approach the original hernia. Another lesson in patience. Had I delayed my departure long enough to experiment with medical treatment for the hiatus hernia, I could have had my gall bladder removed with a laparoscope and saved myself from the whole saga of major open surgery. I did not know that laparoscopic surgery was only a few months away at the time. I wonder why nobody told me.

I had made the decision to leave my old life, but I soon discovered that there are many levels of going forth. Should I let my house or sell it? Should I wind up my business affairs in New Zealand or mothball them? By March 1991, six months after the commitment had been made, I was ready to leave. The house was let, an agent appointed to guard my worldly affairs, and three tearful women, my sister Mary, youngest daughter Liz, and Diane, were lined up by my rose garden to bid me farewell. None of us knew when, or whether, we would meet again. This was no holiday or even reconnaissance. This was going forth, leaving for all time the conditions that were limiting my spiritual progress. It was certainly possible that I would come back to Auckland, even to the same house, but never as the same person with the same responses as before.

It was, as it had been on my trip two years previously, obligatory to travel via Houston, Texas, to visit daughter Susan who, after a packet of adventures since she had left home some six years previously, was now a student at the prestigious Baylor Medical School. Arriving in Houston, I found, was easier than departing. The Gulf War was drawing to a close. Oil wells were burning all over Kuwait. The experts in putting out burning oil wells were, of course, Texans who, in answering an emergency call, were not to be discouraged by such trifles as fully-booked aeroplanes. The airline rose to the occasion by offering booked passengers the equivalent of a thousand New Zealand dollars subsidy on their next flight if they delayed their journey by one day. When Susan found that I intended to transfer it to her next New Zealand holiday she was more than willing to offer me one more night's board and lodging. The following night, as we fronted up to the check-in, the same announcement came over the public address system. At least that was what Susan told me. A Texan accent echoing round an airline terminal was more than my linguistic skill could manage. Once more I volunteered to sacrifice a day for a similar consideration, only to find after a long wait that I was the last passenger to be squeezed onto the plane.

A few days later I was installed in the same little whitewashed stone room that had been my home two years previously at Vajraloka retreat centre in North Wales. Who was I, and what was I doing in this remote valley in a strange land 20,000 kilometres from anybody who had known me for more than a few days or weeks? These questions burned deeper and deeper into my heart until homesickness, longing for friends and family, for Diane, and for Liz, for my little house with its roses and panoramic view of the Hauraki Gulf, for a loving shoulder to rest on, exploded in a tearful call for help. The astonished recipient of all this was Ratnabandhu, a soft-spoken Irish physician and meditation teacher who heard me out with an empathy deep enough to forestall any attempt at helpful advice. As we walked together in a nearby pine forest my bewilderment and grief were washed away, never to return. The first great hurdle had been cleared. The way ahead was open.

Not long after this episode, the retreat centre was struck by an influenza epidemic, which I was not to escape. In spite of a burning fever I found myself meditating in my little white room on a hot afternoon. There came a crash like several thunderstorms, as a fighter plane hurtled overhead close to the speed of sound, so low, it seemed, as to threaten the chimney pots. This was no isolated experience – these valleys were a frequent site for low flying practice. An angry voice, quiet but clearly audible in the back of my head, growled, 'You stupid old goat, sitting there trying to be the Buddha. Why don't you get out there and do something about that evil thing?' Was it a feverish hallucination, or a deep meditation experience? The picture of Avalokitesvara came down from the wall to stand before me and said in a soft, clear voice, 'With gentle, patient persistence, continue with what you're doing.'

I have no memory of my immediate response to this apparition and its advice. I woke in the autumn dusk from a sticky sleep with the realization not only that that machine was a product of the fear and hatred of a society, but that, once spawned, it would breed more of its kind by reinforcing those very emotions from which it had arisen. Some people, like the heroic women staking out the Greenham Common airbase, were already taking very necessary non-violent direct action. I could do something similar, but Avalokitesvara's message was that I should continue working to overcome my own fear and hatred, the better to be able to spread kindness and love throughout the world. My whole past rose in revolt against this apparent passivity, but my emerging understanding knew the counsel to be true. In subsequent years I have held many battles with Provider, as the champion of vigorous activity for the benefit of my tribe, to support the course of putting aside obvious 'things to be done' in favour of continuing with spiritual practice.

It was not all hard work. For a time, a team of New Zealanders was working during the retreat to transform one of the barns into a dining room. In spite of their best efforts, this inevitably caused some disturbance. One bright morning I was part of a class being led through some relaxation exercises before a meditation in the shrine-room. The teacher this day was Vajrachitta, an Irishman soft of voice and softer of heart. 'Now let y'r shoulders fall down y'r back like dey were tied on wid rubber bands.' As he uttered the last word there came from the neighbouring barn a resounding crash. The gentle voice continued, 'Now if dat feller would koindly pick up 'is arrrm we'll go on wid de practice.'

Some months later, at Padmaloka, my enthusiasm and pride caught up with me. Ignoring warnings from teachers, I energetically undertook the six element meditation, which is designed to loosen one's attachment to the body-mind with which the unenlightened person identifies. Just how powerful that practice could be, I was soon to learn. As I sat one morning in the old barn that had recently been converted into a meditation hall, hearing the squirrels cavorting in the ceiling space, and in my imagination vigorously detaching myself from each of the elements of which I was made, a fearful vision arose. From darkness above my head, suspended by a golden cord, descended a great, shining sword, moving closer and closer as it swung in great circles around my body. With each sweep past my fascinated gaze, another layer of habitual behaviours and things from which I had created an identity, my professional status, my house with all its associations, my clothing, even my ideas and views, fell away. Elation rose within me. When this was all gone I would know who I really was. Closer and closer. When would it stop? As it finally came to rest at the centre of my being the terrifying realization broke through. When all of that was shorn away, what was left was … nothing! I had no real identity. I was just a bundle of habits and attachments and nothing else. I can still feel the hair rising on my neck, the prickling of cold sweat on my back, and the fluttering of my heart as this awful truth swept over me. What to do? Where to go to find an identity? Of course, I had long known, behind the eyes, that I had no true identity, but this was knowing in the heart. This was more than a mere abstract knowing: it was direct experience of a truth from which there was no escape.

As the panic subsided, I heard in the back of my head the voice of Priyananda, my guide through my early meditation experiences in Auckland. 'If you hit trouble, don't keep it to yourself. Go and tell somebody.' Who to tell? Who would understand my experience, when to me it was pure chaos? There was no question really. While my mind was frantically questioning, my feet were carrying me towards Subhuti's caravan. Subhuti was to be my preceptor (that is to say, he would in due course conduct my initiation and ordination ceremony). If he didn't understand, nobody would. During the next few days, Subhuti, ever patient, led me to the realization that losing my identification with the self that I had cherished for so long was no tragedy. The only identity I could truly claim was the process of going for refuge to the Buddha, the Dharma, and the Sangha, the ever deepening commitment to the Buddhist ideals for which I had left home all those lifetimes ago. However real my old identity may have felt, and in future moments of doubt would inevitably seem to be again, it was in truth an illusion. For the first time, I found myself coming to terms with the existential paradox of experiencing a self, solid and separate from all other selves, and permanent, yet knowing in my heart that it was in reality only a process, a succession of mind states with no intrinsic identity. I also learned something of the nature of the relationship between teacher and disciple, and even discovering a little humility in the process.

Although I was doing all that I could think of to further my spiritual progress, perhaps impetuously, and with less regard for the advice of my teachers than was good for me, my expanding awareness became more and more fixed on the discomfort of underlying restlessness. The six months that had passed since I shouldered my pack and left my Castor Bay haven had been spent in one retreat centre or another, diligently applying myself to meditation, study, and the new art of reflection. I was learning so much every day. But I was not becoming happier. Sangharakshita had commented, 'If Buddhism is not making you happier, what's the point of it?' So once more I addressed myself to Subhuti with the question, 'I know something is not right. What else should I be doing?' He carefully sifted through the information I offered about my practice to date, then agreed. 'You do seem to be doing the right things. There must be something more that you are not doing.' Now it was obvious. There was nobody in my life who had known me for more than a few months, and I was doing nothing that was of any immediate use to anybody else. I needed to stay in one place to develop closer friendships, and I needed to find some altruistic activity to bring a sense of satisfaction to my days.

In Clapham, not far south of Battersea Bridge in London, was Utpala community, where Mark and Richard were living. Together with most of the other members of the community they travelled each day in a battered Ford Transit van to Croydon, some miles further south, to work in Hockney's Restaurant, part of the Croydon Buddhist Centre complex. I had no desire to take on the long hours of often heavy work that the restaurant demanded, but perhaps the Centre could find a more suitable use for enough of my time and talents to entitle me to a place in the community. My offer to work for three or four days a week without pay as receptionist and bookshop manager was accepted by the centre manager with such alacrity that for a moment I wondered if there was something I had not been told. I need not have worried. It was no more sinister than a chronic shortage of both people and money. So it was that, on 13 September 1991, after a week or two of wandering London sleeping wherever I could find an unoccupied bed, I joined ten other men in Utpala community. As I walked in the door my eye fell on an assortment of bills and love letters scattered on the hall table, among which was an imposing envelope bearing my name and marked urgent and important. It contained the letter from Subhuti inviting me on the 1992 ordination course at Guhyaloka Retreat Centre in Spain.

So I was really to be ordained, and in only a few months. The panic at the prospect was momentary. Others no better prepared than I was had done it and survived. And I was not alone. During the next few weeks three more copies of the letter arrived, addressed to Richard, Mark, and Marcus from Wellington, four New Zealanders to walk this perilous path together.

As I look back to realize it seems incredible that this period of intense study, work, friendship building, meditation, and even writing poetry, lasted only six months. The countdown to our departure for Spain was well under way when Mary phoned. Mother was dying. It was over a year since I had made my farewells to the ancient lady, lying in a hospital bed, suffering progressive dementia as a result of repeated small strokes. There had been a moment of lucidity while I was explaining that I might not see her again. 'You're going away to do something religious. I hope you know what you're doing. But I'll wait for you.' Then a relapse into her private world of long ago. She could not wait for me. Two days before I was to depart from England, choosing a rare moment of solitude, she quietly stopped breathing. I put a portrait of her as she had been in her early twenties on the community shrine, and with my friends sent her all the support I could. There was no real grief. The woman I knew had died long ago.

# 24

# the secret valley

5 a.m. on 6 April 1992. Some two dozen men gathered at Gatwick Airport to board a cheap charter flight to Alicante on the Costa Blanca, en route for Guhyaloka, the fabled 'secret valley'. Such a mixture of emotions. Jocular camaraderie, anxiety, and even fear, the excitement of facing the unknown, all underlain by the brittleness of a night rudely cut short by a 3 a.m. alarm. Waiting by the runway for the roar of engines on full power, accelerating, and lifting from the familiarity of British soil. A crackling voice on the intercom, 'I say chaps, frightfully sorry but we'll have to go back. One of the waggly things on the wing won't waggle.' Two hours later the same voice, 'Sorry, chaps, we've fixed the waggly thing but now the company won't let us use this plane. We'll have to go and find another one.' Perhaps the three hour delay was a good thing. The party that was finally airborne was certainly a much more sober one.

How can I tell of the transformation that began as I entered the secret valley? Physically, we were contained by a deep valley of awful beauty and grandeur high in the limestone mountains, bounded by precipitous cliffs and craggy pinnacles clothed in all manner of prickly vegetation. To enter here was to leave behind the time, space, and events of the familiar world. Time became the rhythm of the daily programme within the span of our sixteen weeks' stay. Mark and I shared one of the fifteen or so tiny huts scattered among the pitch pine, rosemary, and gorse of the valley floor. The setting was ideal for our purpose, which was no less than to shed our old lives and begin anew.

Within a very few days I became aware of a quality of experience quite different from anything I had ever known. The isolation, the grandeur, the programme of meditation, group study, discussion, strange rituals, worship, and walking among these arid peaks, all guided by Subhuti's command of the dramatic, quickly began to strip away old attitudes and behaviours to expose the reality within. Sensitivity to self, to others, to nature, and to the realities of existence, deepened as the need for self-protection dissolved.

Familiarity was never allowed to dilute the process. After five weeks, as I was becoming accustomed to the routine, we were suddenly plunged into silence, punctuated each morning by Subhuti leading the six element meditation, which was designed to break apart one's sense of fixed identity. I had long since lost my main defence of activity and achievement. There was no escape into work. There was no work to do. Now I had lost the defence of speech, which is so often a protection from, rather than an aid to, communication. Hour by hour, day by day, my old patterns of thought and behaviour were being lifted from me. Delight, despair, confidence, fear, elation, depression, confusion, and understanding chased one another round my overexcited mind, each experienced with burning intensity. And on the eighth day of silence I was to face private ordination. As the oldest of the gathering I was to be the first to venture into the unknown and the unknowable.

The six element practice involved identifying with the elements of earth, water, fire, air, space, and consciousness within myself, appreciating that I could in no way own them, but that I had borrowed them from the universe and in due course would give them back. Under the intense conditions of the retreat, all this led to some deep reflections. I quote a small section from my diary:

You towering, awful cliffs, rough, harsh and grey, barren and inhospitable, impervious to the ages, permanence enthroned. Your jagged peaks and jutting crags have defied time since before consciousness began. You mock me in your massive, unshakeable might. Me, a puny creature of the passing moment, ephemeral as the mayfly beneath your scornful pride.

But I feel welcome in my niche on your rough body, nestling against your ancient form. Your face above me is softened, pock-marked with the rains of the ages. You are scarred with cracks and fissures, signs of your great age like the lines and wrinkles on my ageing hands.

Wait. On your surface there is life. Lichens sprawl over your smoother parts, and rust-red mosses. Grasses spring from your fissures, and small red and green succulents nestle in your hollows. Wild flowers smile softly on your shattered surface. In the deeper cracks small shrubs, rosemary, holly oak, even a brave fir tree, find support and sustenance enough for their tiny needs.

And, see – you are not immune to the ages. All about me I see pieces of your substance, as big as my finger or much, much bigger than my body, breaking away from your surface, ready to roll to the valley floor so far below. Yes, like all phenomena, you became and you will pass, giving way to the products of new conditions, which will pass in their turn.

You are as beautiful and welcoming as the face of an ageing mother, or the work-worn hands of a loving grandfather. My fingers reaching to caress your ancient surface thrill to the contact with the wisdom of the ages. I almost sense your stirring in response to my loving touch.

A little green gecko, yellow striped and spotted, darts from a crevice and busily explores the broken rock about me, tiny tongue flicking, sensing I know not what. Now it climbs the grey, broken branches of a long-dead shrub, leaping, agile as a squirrel, from twig to branch. There are ants, and iridescent green beetles, yes, and the steady drone of bees.

My day, the day after the May full-moon celebration of the Buddha's Enlightenment, arrived. I was feted as the hero (or was it the sacrificial victim?) of the day with cakes, flowers, cards, and presents, all offered with smiles and silence. By mid-morning I could stand the emotional tension no longer. Taking my close friend David's hand I led him from the retreat center into the pine forest and promptly burst into noisy tears on his shoulder. After that catharsis and a good hug I was ready to face whatever the day should bring forth. (When it came to his day he did exactly the same to me!)

Subhuti was not through his build-up to the ceremony yet. In the evening puja he launched into a eulogy about some heroic man who was to face private ordination that evening, finishing with the statement, 'When he reaches the branch in the path, if he should choose to take the left branch to the ordination stupa rather than the right branch that leads to Benidorm [a notoriously brash tourist town on the coast some forty kilometres away], it will be because, alone and regardless of what anybody else in the world thinks or does, he chooses death and rebirth rather than returning to his old life. I hope he pauses and thinks deeply before making his choice.' After some consideration I did recognize the man he spoke of – the courage, the commitment, the years of experience from which homespun wisdom had grown, the maturity as evident in my effect on the community, the depth of feeling, including acceptance of such dark feelings as fear, and the acceptance of responsibility, although I was not sure if I carried that as lightly as he said I did. I had these qualities, and was ready to continue to develop them for the benefit of all beings.

I did pause at the branch in the path, not because there was any doubt, but to be sure that I was fully aware of the solemnity of the occasion. I had been facing spiritual death for over a week in the six element practice, which was wearing away my old self, leading me, in fact, to the death of who I thought I was. Now I was facing rebirth in the form of a personal practice that would bring me into direct contact with Reality. This was no occasion to be taken lightly.

The ceremony, although brief and simple, had a significance too deep to be expressed in words. Later that night, as I sat in the tiny room in the stupa reflecting on my life to date, I was totally sure that whatever mistakes I had made in the past, this decision was absolutely right. I had been initiated into the visualization practice of Green Tara, the embodiment of universal compassion expressing itself on earth. And for the rest of this life my name would be Taranatha, which means, on the earthly level, 'protected by Tara', and on the level of aspiration, 'protector of the qualities of Tara'. Most Buddhist names have these two levels of meaning, the first describing who one is now, and the second to act as a goal, a target for one's spiritual endeavours. Both meanings seemed totally appropriate. Somebody had indeed been near to rescue me from one potential disaster after another, and the stimulus to live and exemplify compassion was a perfect vision to guide my path. Now I had sole possession of the stupa for another twenty hours in which to absorb and reflect on all that had happened.

From my diary for 18 May:

How long have I slept? As I open the door to emerge in the predawn, the chorus of nightingales floods over me. The full moon is lying low over the west cliff. There is peace, not soft and woolly, but clear, sharp, and precise as the jagged mountain silhouettes and the nightingales' notes.

The day passes with meditation and reflection in the soft cool light of the stupa, and sitting outside in the hot sun to demolish the massive meals my friends bring me. Breakfast with yoghurt and crusty brown bread, both of which I made yesterday.

5 p.m. Sitting in reflection when the heavens let loose. Not one but two thunderstorms rolling over the north cliff – one to the west and one to the east – and the gap passing right over me!

Crashing, roaring, rolling thunder, jagged lightning darting all round, and two drops of rain on me.

Back to the silent retreat – but I suddenly feel crowded in the presence of thirty-two other men, albeit silent ones. Exhausted, as if soaked, wrung out, and draped over a rail to dry, and two and a half hours in the shrine-room before I can rest. But I want to be there for Simon [the next man to go to the stupa].

There had been eight days of total silence. Now I found myself back among my friends, bearing a name that none of them had heard, and facing a further twenty-eight days of silence to be maintained within the bounds of the retreat. If it was absolutely necessary to speak we were asked to move out of earshot of the buildings, which in an enclosed valley shaped like a shell was a long way. Each day another man was celebrated as man of the day – all in silence. Each evening another man left the shrine-room to take that perilous path through the scrub to the stupa, to return the following evening a different being.

Four weeks had passed since I became Taranatha, four weeks of maintained and even deepening intensity. The culmination of the retreat was to be the public ordination, an all-day ceremony in which twenty-six men were to be welcomed into the Western Buddhist Order, their names would be announced, and, ominously, the silence would be broken. A further quote from my diary:

12.15 p.m. The bell, and in we troop. Our (old) names are stuck on the floor to mark our places – in size and position exactly between what I can see with reading glasses and without. Help! It comes, and Maharatnapriya leads me to my place.

Pictures of old friends and relatives line the walls. By my right shoulder, Diane, Priyananda, and Dharmadhara. Across the room all five daughters watch with interest. My response? Tears, of course.

The long lead-in.... Three parts to the ceremony, in all of which I have to go first and find out how to do it. The offerings, flowers, candle, and incense, the consecrated water on the head, and finally the kesa [the broad ribbon of white silk worn round the neck as a symbol of commitment] planted firmly and momentarily held in place. By this time I am red-eyed and stuffy-nosed, having been fully engaged with the whole proceeding. So now I am a Dhammachari [a follower of the Buddha's teaching], and all thought of escape is far gone.

It has been a long and eventful trip to this point. And Diane is very much here. The Green Tara and the White Tara on the shrine came from her, the cushion I sit on, and the picture on the wall. And the kesa wallet waiting for its occupant.

A tea break. Sanghadeva serving tea and cakes while we sit with our experience, then the naming. Subhuti talks for three hours, with no sign of waning inspiration. Again, I am first, TARANATHA. So much is said, but the little bits that matter are, 'In spite of his best efforts, this man has been quite unable to foul up his life enough to make him unfit to join the Order. *Somebody's* been looking after him!' and 'All he has to do is stop struggling, let himself become Tara, and let it all happen.' Let go and let Tara – that is the way for the rest of this life.

Various rituals, including a superb three-course dinner during which the thirty-seven-day silence was formally ended, continued into the evening, until:

A bit bewildered, to bed at 10.30, to sleep, to dream, to wake, and to sleep again. Hanging in the window is a crystal given by a friend. At 4.10 a.m., which I am told is exactly full moon, I am woken by a beam of emerald-green light, the colour of the light radiated by Tara – the full moon via the crystal – in the left eye.

The stage management of this retreat was superb. Although the build-up with its culmination in the public ordination had been reached at ten weeks, with a further six weeks to go there was no sense of anticlimax as we moved into the next phase, learning to be Order members. As day followed day so many teachings appeared, in the course of formal study, in casual conversation, or just in the example of somebody's ethical behaviour. One profoundly simple teaching that has influenced my life ever since happened as I was walking a mountain track with Subhuti. Memory still sees brave little wild flowers clinging to a pale grey limestone outcrop to my left, the path ahead skirting an ancient olive grove, and a glowering cliff beyond an expanse of rocky wilderness to the right.

'You seem to do the work of three men,' I said to him, 'yet you always look relaxed and cheerful. How do you do it?'

In a voice of innocent surprise he replied, 'Well, I do what I'm doing... and then I do the next thing.' Which, after a moment of reflection, I realized was exactly the way he lived. He did what he was doing, be it building a Buddhist centre, teaching the Dharma, walking with me, or eating his lunch, fully present, aware, concentrated, and therefore happy. When he had finished one activity he put it down and took up the next, present, aware, concentrated, and happy. I did not live that way, and in spite of having made some progress, I still don't.

When the end came into sight, a few days before we were to leave the valley, a deliberate programme of relaxation was instituted. Some of the men even hitched a ride with the support team members to visit Sella, a hill town some eleven kilometres away. The final event of the retreat was the speakers' school, in which each of us gave a half-hour talk to the assembled Order, now numbering thirty-two members, on some aspect of the Dharma. Although most of us found this something of an ordeal, some of the talks were so striking that I still remember them. My own contribution was on the theme of craving and addiction, drawing on my experience of alcoholism, addictive disease in general, and the 'normal' experience of craving as illustrated by the attachment most of us had shown for the fresh brown bread that I had helped to bake every other day for sixteen weeks.

The adventure was over. The day came for us to leave the valley and return to England. With three of my friends I decided that leaving in a Land Rover was not appropriate after such a mythic journey. Accordingly, having tossed our packs on the waiting vehicle, we set off in the blistering heat to walk to Sella, where our coach waited to take us to the airport. One of the attractions of this plan was a pool of clear, cold water fed by a mountain spring, which we were told we would pass on the way. Having not seen standing water since we left the coast we were more than enthused about taking a dip. I have no idea what the water temperature was, but I'll not forget the shock as I cheerfully jumped into it. Apparently the heat of the summer sun does not penetrate the depths of the mountain whence this water came.

From the diary:

Coda. The plane climbs eastwards over the Mediterranean, then, as if drawn by the magic of Guhyaloka, swings round to the north in perfect position to show the valley laid out below. There are the shrine-room, dining room, huts, even the stupa, and the tracks that I walked so often, radiating out over the mountains. It is a fitting finale to the myth that is Guhyaloka.

# 25

# the return journey

I had been told many times that the man who returned to London would be a different being from the man who had left it sixteen weeks earlier. I had heard and heeded the words. I was shattered when I found how different. Smiling as bravely as I could through the boisterous receptions, first at the airport and then (it was 2 a.m. by the time we reached Clapham) at Utpala community, I retreated in a state of confusion to my little room. For two or three days I hovered between the haven of my room and the enclosed garden, meeting others only at mealtimes, and then as briefly as possible. Samamati (ex-Mark) and Akashagarbha (ex-Marcus) had gone straight back to work at the Croydon Buddhist Centre, while Sagaravajra (ex-Richard) had joined the team at Rivendell, a retreat centre in the soft Sussex countryside. Eventually, knowing I could hide no longer, I walked, eyes lowered to the littered pavement 'a plough's length' ahead of me, the familiar route along Balham High Street to catch the dingy train to Croydon. Eight miles, mostly between rows of tiny back yards of sooty brick tenements. At least, since it was summer, the same sad washing was not displayed day after day forlornly seeking to dry, as it had been before I left.

Summer it was indeed. Decanted at Croydon, I emerged from the station into a steamy hot August morning in the High Street, now no longer a highway but a crowded pedestrian mall. All about me, women walking proud and shapely, wearing a minimum of clothing, designed to reveal rather than to conceal. A honey-blonde princess seen in a shop window bending towards me to try on a shoe, her ample breasts barely controlled by a skimpy top. Long legs surmounted by tiny skirts struggling to contain firm, round buttocks. This was disturbing, but less so than I had feared. These were normal human beings proudly displaying their confident bodies – all quite healthy.

Finding downcast eyes no protection, I looked up to be confronted by the horrors of exploitation, mostly brash sexual exploitation, in advertisements on hoardings and in shop windows. There was no escape. Each new view as I hurried towards the safety of the Buddhist Centre was another human image selling its humanity to commerce. After an age (it was no more than ten minutes) I dived into the sanctuary of the Centre, to collapse in the familiar swivel chair behind the familiar worn and friendly desk. There, surmounted by a card, 'WELCOME HOME, TARANATHA. Can you sort this lot out?' was a stack of books and papers. A new edition with the cover upside-down, a stack of new books with no invoice, an invoice with no books, a bundle of requests for books to be ordered, and an assortment of one-off problems. For a time I could only stare, then from somewhere deep inside a silent scream of pain, 'No! No! I can't do this! I can't! I won't! All my life I've driven myself to do things and I won't do it any more!'

Where to go? What to do? There was nothing for it but to brave the street and the train again and scuttle back to the protection of my solitary room and the company of the squirrels in the garden. At the community I found a letter from Mary enclosing an abstract from Joseph Campbell's *The Hero's Journey*, graphically describing the difficulties of the hero's return home after his successful quest for the 'treasure'. Somebody knew about all of this. Somebody understood. It was not only the famous mythologist Joseph Campbell who understood what I was suffering. Since Mary had seen fit to send it, she must have had some understanding too.

It was good to read Campbell's description of the whole of the hero's journey, appearing in one form or another, so he said, in all world cultures. First, the Call, that barely audible voice that whispers, 'Is this what life's all about? Is there no more to it than this?' Of the many descriptions of the Call that appear in the world's mythologies, perhaps the most beautiful is the Hindu story of the *gopis*, the cowgirls, drawn by haunting tones of Krishna's flute drifting from the jungle in the dead of night, rising from their beds to enter the fearful darkness and dance with Krishna. Then follows the Quest, the dangerous journey in search of the Treasure, guarded by a fearful dragon or equally terrifying monster. Overcoming the guardian, by force, guile, or persuasion, constitutes the Ordeal, by which the hero's fitness to possess the treasure is tested. Finally, having secured the treasure, the hero faces the Return Journey, which, far from being a happy homecoming may be the most challenging episode in the whole drama. Returning triumphant to offer the treasure to the world, the hero finds that nobody is interested in it. In fact, since the treasure is something that threatens to change them, the people actively refuse to have anything to do with it, or with the hero in his new form. All this was so familiar to me, so exactly describing the journey I had been following with increasing intensity for the past few years. It almost seemed that claiming the treasure had made me unfit to resume life in the world that I had long since left.

I gradually began to come to terms with the 'real' world, the crowds in the streets, the harshness, the exploitation, the constant display of sex, even the stack of problems on the desk, but I knew it could not be sustained. Diane had left New Zealand not long after me to join a Buddhist publishing business in Glasgow. She, too, was having difficulties. Glasgow was a long way from South London, but at least it was on the same side of the world and on the same piece of land. Perhaps we could meet, walk in the country, and share our troubles. So with a phone call or two it was arranged. She would hire a small car to drive south while I would find a fast train heading north to meet her in Penrith. From there we would wend our way into the Lake District to comfort our aching hearts with friendship and the beauty of nature.

A few days later, as I sat in silence beside my dear friend on a crag overlooking the crazy little road of Honister Pass, peace found me. With the silence and the rugged beauty of the mountains and lakes came understanding. In those sixteen weeks at Guhyaloka I had developed a tender sensitivity that far outstripped the slowly growing equanimity necessary to support it. At this moment my heart was ecstatically opening to silence, beauty, and friendship. For the past few weeks, defenceless, it had been bruised and torn by the pervading harshness of the city.

The diagnosis was plain, but where to seek the remedy for this painful malady? Determined though I was to protect my new-found sensitivity, I knew it would be years before equanimity could grow to match it. I could not sit on a peak in the Lake District to wait for it, I was in no shape to stay long-term in London, and I needed more experience with the Order in Britain before I would be ready to go back to New Zealand. In search of comfort, I had even sought to resume our sexual relationship which we had suspended nearly a year earlier, to find Diane gently insisting that that would bring more difficulties than it could solve. Having tasted the freedom of living for months with a vow of chastity I knew she was right, but in my present distress I could not pretend to welcome her determination. It was with a deeply troubled mind that I sat watching the autumn countryside flashing past the train window a few days later. Again Tara was looking after me. A message in the hall at the community, 'Call Sagaravajra at Rivendell. Urgent.' His friendly voice on the phone, 'Glad you're back. A man's leaving here next week and we need a replacement. Come and join us.'

# 26

# rivendell

In my battered state, Rivendell looked like a paradise. The soft beauty of the East Sussex countryside, a patchwork of forest, pasture, and cultivated fields spreading over low, rolling hills. Ancient brick or sandstone farmhouses with a scattering of modern, tastefully opulent stockbroker residences. Narrow, winding lanes, trimmed hawthorn hedges and dry-stone walls, and a network of public footpaths making it all accessible. Then there was Rivendell itself, a lovely mid-Victorian brick house set in two hectares of garden and forest, home to an uncountable variety of birds and endemic wild life, squirrel, rabbit, fox, badger, all manner of small rodents and the grass snake and adder that preyed upon them. The property had been a rectory in the tiny village of High Hurstwood. The neighbouring stone church with its small graveyard now served a much smaller congregation than it had apparently done in its beginnings. Although it was not immediately apparent on the ground, it was obvious from the map that the public footpaths, now tramped by hikers rather than worshippers, converged on the church from the far reaches of the parish.

I fell in love with the house at first sight. Two-storeyed, high gabled with tall chimneys of fancy brickwork, massive wooden doors with wrought-iron fittings, external walls of ancient brick or locally-made tiles, it was a picture of rural elegance. Presumably some of the nine bedrooms had been for the servants, but it did appear that rectors were expected to be a fecund lot.

The interior had been modernized to house, feed, and entertain up to two dozen retreatants, in considerably more comfort than could be claimed by the resident team. Our quarters, squeezed into one end of an outbuilding, most of which had been given to a meditation hall, were a little daunting at first sight. I was initially offered a corner of the tiny living room, virtually a corridor, in which to set up a bed I had found in a garden shed. In due course I found an unoccupied nook between a chimney and a hot-water cylinder under the roof of the mediation hall which, with the aid of several volunteers of various skills, I converted into a tiny bedroom. Long enough for a bed and a desk, high enough under the middle third of the pitched roof for me to stand, and just wide enough for me to walk past the bed to the desk, it could never have been called luxurious, but it was my own space into which I could retreat and shut the door. Two features I particularly enjoyed. One of the long walls, following an adjoining roof line, sloped steeply away to give an illusion of spaciousness, and the opening skylight under which, if I moved the chair aside, I could stand with my head above the roof, enjoying the highly civilized view.

Most important of all were the men with whom I would be living and working. Sagaravajra, with whom I had studied in Auckland and Croydon, Priyadarsin from Stockholm who had gone through the fire of the ordination process with Sagaravajra and me, and Viryabodhi, also from Stockholm, with whom I had started a friendship at Croydon. Three of us new to the Order, and the fourth only two years older. Chronologically, each of the others was not far short of half my age, but somehow that did not seem to be important, at least to me. All of us were fired with the enthusiasm of the recently ordained to make Rivendell work for the Dharma as no retreat centre had ever done before.

Rivendell and I did indeed meet each other's needs. I found beauty, quiet, friendship, and a welcome for my enthusiasm to share the Dharma. In me, the house found a loving caretaker, and the team a relatively mature and steadying influence. Mr Busy-Fix-It was in his element, granted full control of my energies for at least a part of most days. So many maintenance jobs to be done. A few tiles missing from a wall by the front door, the kitchen drain to be cleared, dry rot to be cut from a window sill and the gaping hole filled. The community transport, a venerable Volvo wagon, to be patched, rewired, nurtured, and sometimes bullied into ferrying our supplies from farm markets and our guests from Buxted railway station, a couple of miles away. As my sense of identitification with the house grew, I undertook more ambitious projects, culminating in building a commercial washing machine and dryer into a tiny out-house. The space was so small that the appliances could be operated only with the doors wide open, the operator standing outside in the weather, but it did allow us to have the house fully prepared for the next retreat within hours of the departure of the last one.

Even such an idyllic lifestyle had its hazards. Since most of our retreats catered for people of both sexes who were relatively new to Buddhism, it was inevitable that some of our more naive guests would see retreat leaders as enlightened gurus. Inexperienced teachers, especially if young and celibate, could so easily mistake expressions of wide-eyed adoration, especially on the faces of young, attractive women, for something much more mundane. When the adoring student made the same mistake, the stage was set for a much-ado-about-nothing drama. Condescendingly, I sympathized with my young colleagues over their dilemmas, until I found that most retreats included at least one middle-aged woman, widow, divorcee or, worst of all, one in the midst of marital difficulties, turning those same adoring eyes onto me! Well aware as I was of my craving for intimacy, I narrowly avoided more than one potentially disastrous situation.

When the crash came, it was from a different direction. I suppose it was inevitable. As our enthusiasm spread through the pool of potential guests, Rivendell's popularity grew, and with it our workload. With unlimited opportunity for pouring energy into such inspiring and usually enjoyable activity, I drove myself to exhaustion. The crisis came while I was cooking for a full retreat in which I was not personally involved. It was a formula for loneliness, being in the presence of others communicating deeply with each other but not with me. Anxious work, catering for twenty-five guests, demanding great results from primitive skills. One evening, as I was serving dinner, I felt my scalp shrinking. Tighter and tighter was the grip in my skull, more and more remote my grip on what I was doing, until I found myself standing in paralysed indecision in the kitchen, unable to think what serving dishes to use or where to find them. A step or two ahead of the advancing panic, Viryabodhi appeared. 'You don't look well, Taranatha. Let me serve the dinner.' Out into the summer evening I fled, to wander the lonely footpaths through the healing beauty of fields and forest until the failing light drove me home.

It was with an overwhelming sense of failure that I approached the community meeting the following morning. Only my persisting two-sizes-too-small scalp convinced me that I was not shirking, and that something was profoundly wrong. My friends had already assessed the situation and were in no mood for argument. 'Daphne and Bill want to go away for two weeks. We've told them you will look after the cottage and dog. When you come back we'll have shared out most of your duties and you are to take it easy.' My immediate indignant response, 'Cheeky young pups. Who do you think you're organizing?' faded before it was spoken. My three friends were determined in their kindness and understanding – and they were obviously right.

Daphne and Bill, regular attenders at our Tuesday evening meditation group, lived in an eighteenth-century cottage in Hartfield, a nearby village in the heart of Winnie-the-Pooh country. For two weeks I slept, listened to music from Daphne's record collection, and took the dog exploring the footpaths through Hundred Acre Wood, stopping now and then to greet ghosts from Christopher Robin's nursery or to play Poohsticks at Poohsticks Bridge.

These walks gave me opportunities to reflect on what had led to my being here, recuperating from what was popularly called burn-out. How had I let myself drift into such a state? What drove me to work beyond my capacity, and why didn't I notice the symptoms while I was still able to make changes? It seemed to have something to do with enjoyment. Driving myself to achieve bought acceptance and love. Enjoying what I was doing was play, which had little or no purchasing power. How humiliating to find that after five or six years of meditation I was only now discovering that I was stuck in childhood conditioning! The answer? Continue to be helpful wherever I could, but consciously in the service of my highest ideal (personified by Tara) rather than unconsciously to gain approval. Seek enjoyment in whatever I was doing and watch for early symptoms of exhaustion. While learning these skills, rely on my friends to monitor my activity. It might seem incredible that such simple understanding could be so far to seek, but that is the nature of early conditioning. Behaviours learned so long ago were protective, even life-saving, not lightly to be challenged.

I had already decided that I would return to New Zealand within a year or two. When I undertook to stay for at least a year, I suspect that in the back of my mind was the thought that it would not take much longer than that to prepare me for the relatively rugged conditions for spiritual practice that I would find in Auckland. There were so many Order members in England that they really did not need me, and so few in New Zealand, trying to do so much. But the real reason, as I rather lamely told Subhuti in reply to his challenge, was 'It's home.' True pilgrims have gone beyond attachment to home – apparently I had not. For whatever reason, in the middle of 1993 I gave notice that I would leave at the end of the year. The final deciding factor was the growing realization that Rivendell and the East Sussex countryside were just too civilized, too developed, too softly beautiful to feed the fire in my belly. I was beginning to yearn for the challenge of more pioneering conditions. And so it was that in the first chill of the Sussex winter I set off to visit our two centres in the USA and to meet Susan in Texas again. First a week at Aryaloka Retreat Center near Boston, where the beavers were breaking ice on the dam, then via a full day's flight for another week at Missoula, Montana, where footprints of cougar, black bear, and elk dug deep into the snow. And finally to a week of walking with Susan in the steamy jungles of Costa Rica before returning to my little house at Castor Bay almost three years after I had left it.

# 27

# communities

My return to Castor Bay early in 1994 was in some ways reminiscent of my first arrival thirty-five years earlier. I was then a young, idealistic doctor emerging from years of training as an undergraduate and later as a member of a resident team, determined to devote myself single-handedly to the suffering sick. Now I was an eighteen-month-old Dhammachari, more idealistic than ever, emerging again from training and practice in a residential team, intent on bringing the word of the Buddha to the suffering ignorant. There were two projects that had fired my imagination. The first was to acquire a big house somewhere near the Buddhist Centre in which to establish a men's community, and the second to help to develop the retreat land in the Tararu Valley that Satyananda and others from the Auckland sangha had bought while I was at Rivendell.

From the convergence of Buddhist ideals and the social mores of the sixties and seventies, the custom of living together in communities had arisen quite naturally. Rather to the surprise of the people involved, a number of communities drifted into being, some exclusively for men and some for women. As places for spiritual practice they seemed to work better that way. I had been vaguely thinking that living in a community could be right for me, when the crisis of three years previously that shattered my sense of identity dropped me neatly into Utpala in Clapham. This had been no Utopia set up for my benefit. It was a motley group of eleven men in a large, semi-detached brick house in what had once been a respectable, middle-class Edwardian suburb. I'd had the good fortune to secure a tiny single room on the top floor with a foreground view of a grimy brick chimney, usually surmounted by a ragged grey crow that croaked dismally at the grey sky, standing in a field of grey tiled roofs. My fellow residents had mostly been young, intense, and each in his own way slightly crazy, which included the three New Zealanders with whom I had studied, meditated, and in due course been ordained. This was what men's communities were about: friendship and mutual support on the Buddhist path.

At Rivendell the following year I was to meet these qualities developed to a much higher level.

In the Auckland sangha, single-sex communities had come and gone for twenty years or more, but they had never had the advantage of owning their premises. I would change all that!

First, I had to to re-establish myself as a New Zealander. It was so easy just to walk back into the house that I had walked out of only three years ago. The house, its rose garden, and the breath-taking view, were much the same as when I had left them. It was in trying to fit myself back into that familiar environment that I discovered both the extent of the changes that had taken place in me, and the fragility of the new values and attitudes I had acquired. Friends and family again called in for tea and a chat, neighbours met me in the street with, 'Morning, Doc,' and local shopkeepers greeted me with, 'Good to see you back, Doc.' But I was no longer Doc. The man who was back was not the man who had left. Within a few weeks I found myself fighting to protect my new identity from the siren voices of my old life. Fighting and not winning. The need to change my lifestyle from that of solitary householder to a member of a men's Buddhist community was becoming urgent.

Here arose a difficulty. Dharmadhara and Guhyasiddhi, the two members of the Order with whom I had expected to join forces, having had some difficulties in their community, both decided they needed to live alone for a while. This was a serious setback. I could not continue to make progress on my chosen path while living alone, and the only lifestyle that I knew would suit me was being snatched from me by two men who had other needs. Returning to England was a possibility, but not one that I met with much enthusiasm. However, it was my announcement of this prospect that tipped the balance. Auckland was desperately short of Order members, and if moving in with me was what it took to keep me here, then these men would make the sacrifice. Two other small inducements were that the rented house in which they were living had suddenly been sold, leaving them homeless, and that since I need charge them only living expenses, moving into my house was a relatively cheap option.

So came into being the community that soon acquired the name Mettavihara, 'abode of friendship'. Beginning with known historical tensions, not to mention a host of unknown prospective difficulties, an abode of friendship it had to become if the community, and indeed the men's activities of the Auckland Buddhist Centre, were to survive and flourish. We three, the only men who would regularly be seen leading classes and events at the Centre, were well aware that a genuine and visible friendship between us was an essential ingredient in what we could offer. Friendship does not just happen. It has to arise from a commitment to communication and meeting regularly. In fact, for the whole of the twenty months that we lived in that house, we met every morning after breakfast to discuss plans and to give voice to any difficulties, as well as our appreciation of each other's attainments.

After a year or so, it became obvious that we needed to expand. Akashagarbha had set up home in a caravan in the garden, so there were now four of us. The little house was not only uncomfortably crowded, it was too far from the Centre for people to come home for dinner and get back for an evening meeting. The evening meal was an important community ritual that lost its significance if any of us were absent regularly. We held meetings, so many meetings, of the men in our sangha who had any interest in our lifestyle. The plan was that I would sell the house and set up a trust to buy a property to house a community of six to eight. Eventually, six men committed themselves to the project and agreed on a formidable list of requirements for the new property. And there the project stalled. The list was so exacting, the prospect for meeting its demands so unlikely, and we were all so busy.

In the meantime, I had my own demons to coax out of their dens, befriend, and transform. Far from banishing old habits and prejudices, an intense entry into the spiritual life, at least initially, only brings them out of hiding. My addiction to activity, achievement, and taking responsibility for the world rather than my own mind states had begun to make itself known at Guhyaloka, where there was no 'work' to protect me from awareness of restlessness and the urge to be doing. Now I was back in my old environment, crowded with ghosts of old attitudes and behaviours, and struggling to protect my tender new stillness and contentment. It was a losing battle. So much to be done, and all of it so virtuous! So many responsibilities to take up: developing the community, leading classes, study groups, and retreats, supporting the retreat centre project at Tararu, maintaining the properties of community and centre, and attending meetings of the trusts that administered them. There was no end to opportunities to be busy. My old friend Provider was coming back into his own. Provider, the archetype of the masculine, determined, practical, achieving, materialistic, assertive, and insensitive, reclaiming all that had been taken over by the feminine: the intuitive, imaginative, receptive, and empathic.

From time to time I escaped for a few days to the cottage at Kawau Island to breathe the clean air of beach and bush, away from telephones and the crowded diary of appointments. Each time I sank into the peace of solitude, the busy, driving attitudes of city life gently slipped away, releasing the joy of beauty and quiet contemplation. I found it took three to five days for the image of beauty, initially registering in the mind as interesting or faintly pleasing, to penetrate the depths of the heart as profoundly joyful, even tearfully so. And with each visit the ghosts of the children who had spent so many holidays there became more accepting of my new identity.

If the community were to develop as planned, finding it a more suitable home could not be deferred for ever. In August 1995 I returned, fired with enthusiasm, from Rivendell, where I had attended a reunion with the men with whom I had been ordained. It had been an idyllic week in the old house, with the soft Sussex beauty, and the magical communion with the men with whom I had gone through the fire of transformation. Back at Mettavihara, we were all agreed that the search for a house must begin in earnest. Rather more reluctantly, I agreed that I was the only one available to do it. This was exactly the situation that could send the much mellowed Provider spinning back into his old harsh, guilt-driven self. And it did. Three months of increasingly desperate searching eventually came up with the unbelievable, a property meeting all eight of the criteria we had so lightly decided upon all those lifetimes ago. Three months of increasingly obsessional application to the job in hand left me anxious and, I suspect, impossible to live with. All that remained was to acquire the property, and to do that without incurring a crippling debt.

Onto the scene came Robbie, father of a friend of a friend, a retired auctioneer who had spent most of his life auctioning smallholdings in his homeland of Ireland. As we drove to the auction, Robbie explained to me what was likely to happen. 'If you win the bid, you won't make the reserve and the auctioneer will take you into a back room and try to make you put your price up. Don't be in a hurry!' After some more of this line of advice I said, 'Robbie, this isn't my country. You do the bidding and you talk to the auctioneer if we get into that back room.' That was the best decision I could have made. There was quite a crowd at the house. Robbie surveyed them with his expert eye and pronounced, 'The old Indian lady is the only other bidder here. If she's got more money than you she'll buy it for her family,' and he pointed out the family members all round the room. He was exactly right. The elderly lady placed her bids quickly and confidently. Robbie, leaning against the door, looking out the window and apparently taking little interest in proceedings, casually dropped each bid a second before the auctioneer's hand hit his notebook. He finally won – but he had reached my limit except for a mere five thousand dollars that we had agreed I could spend if it was the only possible way to secure the property. Just as Robbie had predicted, we were herded into a back room, for the auctioneer, a young man apparently unaware that he was totally outclassed by a master, to harangue us into increasing our bid to meet the reserve. For all of twenty minutes this charade went on, the increasingly frantic young man persuading, to be met with the incredulous, 'But that's our bid, for why would we be wantin' to increase it?' Finally, when he had strung it as far as it would go, Robbie played his joker, 'Och, well, we'll give you de odd foive t'ousand.' What pleasure it is to watch a master practise his craft! Off scuttled the auctioneer to persuade the vendor, with more success than he had had with Robbie, that he should lower his reserve to meet us.

We had bought a house. Two houses, in fact, on the same piece of land. Only one hurdle remained. To buy at auction I had signed an unconditional contract, but I had not yet sold my house to raise the alarming amount of money to which I had committed myself. Not without some drama and comedy, this was achieved on the day the payment was due. By the time we were due to move in, my friends decided they could do the job better without an elderly, anxious, and exhausted team member to look after, and bundled me off to Kawau to recuperate while they got on with it. Of course, I did not trust them to do it without me, but I was in no position to argue.

This was not the first property deal with which I had been involved that year. My old medical partners, having decided it was time they owned their rooms instead of renting them from me, had sent me a negotiator to arrange a contract. He led the discussion in the only way he knew, by setting us up as adversaries. Finding he was making no headway with his suggestions, he eventually, in some exasperation, asked, 'If you can't accept anything I propose, what do you want me to do?'

'I'd like you to take a holiday while I go and have a cup of tea with these people. I think we can arrange a deal to our mutual advantage.'

When I met my ex-colleagues in my old office, we had such a contract sorted out in about ten minutes, much to their astonishment. All it took was mutual respect and a little goodwill, qualities that seem only too rare in human interaction. But I confess that I, too, was impressed with the contrast in effectiveness between the adversarial and the friendly methods of negotiation.

The end of 1995 saw us settling into our new community, in which I imagined a future of riding on the wave of the spiritual enthusiasm of my younger friends. In the event it has not been quite like that. Impermanence is a fact of life that applies to communities as much as to everything else. Members arrive and then move on more committed or less committed to the Buddhist path. Numbers have varied over the years from eight to three. But with rare exceptions everyone has at least been committed to living as ethically as they can, which has made for a community spirit that has been, if not ideal, at least pleasant and friendly. For that, I am grateful. Nobody can tell the future, but my wish is that this community should be my last home.

# 28

# a buddhist in the city ...

The changed man who returned after three years of travels was still a tender plant not yet weaned from the hot-house. That I could not keep up my spiritual progress or even resist the 'gravitational pull' of my old life without the support of a community I had discovered very quickly. It took not a lot longer to find that even with that support, establishing myself as an effective member of the Order while in my old environment was a daunting task.

The essential problem was the ingenuity of Provider in keeping himself in work. Not that he didn't take part in all the changes. He took Surata's comment about having the whole world to provide for very seriously, and went to it with a will. The result was that I found myself as busy as I had even been, but instead of tending the sick day and night, I was leading classes and retreats, attending meetings, and seeking responsibilities wherever they were offered. Without doubt there was an altruistic element in all this, but there was also constant nourishment for a hungry ego. In my diaries of those first few years back in Auckland are many anguished entries of the battles between the relentless activity of Provider, powered largely by his driving need to get things done, and the stillness of Tara's compassion arising spontaneously from her insight into Reality.

These conflicts came to be acted out especially on the New Year retreats, in the course of which we ritually burned a confession or a symbol of some aspect of ourselves that we did not want to take forward into the coming year. It was on New Year's Eve 1994, while I was leading a retreat at Awhitu on the Manukau Harbour, that the thought arose that I should offer Provider's hat to the consuming fire, the miner's cap with the narrow-beamed light that always pointed towards the goal and prevented deviation. It is hard to convey the immense significance of this sacrifice in my life as it was at that time. A quote from the diary may help.

1 January 1995. What self-denying labour Provider has given to his world. How he has been ruled by the hat he made for

himself, the hard hat with the narrow-beamed light. And now, hero that he is, he has burned the hat in the presence of the Buddhas. Provider, I bow before your commitment to moving from the familiar refuge of reason and discipline, to venture through the quicksands of uncertainty, groping blindly towards Insight, the source of spontaneity. May all gods protect you, guide you, and encourage you in your quest. May the light of Tara's smile be ever before you, beckoning you on towards Compassion. May total integration be your destination, and compassionate action your achievement.

And the next day:

THE GAP. The chasm between Provider and Tara is coming into awful view. The awe is not so much in its width – slender bridges have already been thrown over it – as in its depth. This is not just a defect in my development. This is an existential split, the split between self and other, the primal separation.

It was five years ago next month that the conflict first became conscious. Provider came into my life as the embodiment of the masculine forces that drove me. Tough, capable, achieving, not for his own glory but for the benefit of those near him. Not only did he provide for self and family, he drove himself day and night to provide for the sick and suffering. In the unconscious recesses of his driving mind there was a spark of true compassion in what he did. His joy was truly, at least in part, the joy of relieving suffering, of helping the crippled to stand and walk.

Over the years provider has grown into a major personality, increasingly aware of himself, his compassion, and his driving energy. Gaining more from his achievement as he becomes more aware of himself and his purpose. Increasingly aware of his pain as the chasm between himself and Reality becomes clearer. Applying increasingly effectively the only force he knows to bridging that gap. But he was limited by the miner's cap, the hard, protective crown with narrow-beamed, penetrating light.

The forces he knows can create bridges over the gap, but they are powerless to heal the awful chasm below. In fact, the very bridges may in some way prevent its closing.

Provider becomes more aware of his own powers, of the existential separation, and of the disparity between the two. Deeper and deeper becomes his understanding, not only that closing this gap is beyond his ability, but that there is a force of Reality that will close it. Now his true heroism is appearing. He becomes willing to sacrifice himself, to lose his identity in giving his strength to that Reality. Two days ago he symbolized that sacrifice by burning his cap.

As I contemplate that act, I am lost in admiration. This is true heroism, the gift of one's very existence for the good of all beings, transcendence of the protective walls of self.

Each time reflection takes understanding a little further, I have a satisfied feeling. 'That's sorted that one out!' So it has, until my meditative mind picks it up again. A symbol as fundamental to my progress as the chasm between Provider and Tara has frequently recurred, each time allowing a slightly deeper glimpse into its mystery.

Provider and Fountain were siblings, born of the same process. Each embodied an unknown, unintegrated aspect of my personality. Both walked with me to the top of the Mythical Mountain, there to discover their archetypal origins. And there their paths diverged. Fountain was newborn, newly-discovered energy, soft, pliant, and ripe for transformation. When she discovered that she was Tara, albeit in a relatively primitive form, she was able to relinquish her previous identity and give herself totally to her new form. In quite a short time Fountain existed only in memory. Her further development as Tara belongs to chapter 30. My life in the city has been much more concerned with Provider.

Provider's transformation was quite a different matter. Having taken the major responsibility for guiding my life since early childhood, he had developed into a resilient, mature, and complex personality. The revelation of his archetypal form as Avalokitesvara set up a serious conflict for him. He could appreciate and admire Avalokitesvara, but so firmly bound was he in his own personality he could not make the transformation. Yet he has come to know that this is exactly what, eventually, he must do, and with that knowledge has come the first glimpse of understanding into how he must do it. It can only happen through progressively giving up the identity he has built over so many years, and allowing himself to be absorbed into Tara. And he has no illusions about how difficult, protracted, painful, and ultimately totally satisfying this process will be. Provider is not accustomed to failure. However many lifetimes it takes him, he will succeed.

I confess that when I emerge from periods of relating to these archetypal figures, whether they be, like Provider, mundane forces clearly from within myself, or more refined, even transcendental, beings like Tara, I wonder whether others not accustomed to this sort of practice would question my sanity. There have been times when I have questioned it myself. I can only report these experiences, as I did the dramatic encounter with Avalokitesvara (chapter 18), as honestly and simply as possible and leave readers to come to their own conclusions.

The days and months of 'just pressing on with practice' set the stage for occasional more dramatic episodes, small breakthroughs of understanding, beginning the meditation on loving kindness, gently fanning a spark of goodwill for myself into a vigorous flame. Suddenly, again for the briefest moment, the experience of total, unconditional appreciation and love for myself. In that moment the realization that in that state I could meet others only with love, that every negative feeling for anybody was no more than a reflection of lack of acceptance of myself. Another demon discovered, to be befriended and transformed over the years.

• A dream in which Jayasri, an Order member of long standing, was jeering at me because she had managed to steal my money. Reflecting on this, I realized that Jayasri symbolized the Order that had 'stolen' my security, represented by my giving my house and a large part of my savings to the Buddhist movement before I had overcome attachment to it.

• Reflection on generosity. This time slowly emerging from the depths, the realization that while I believe I own something, that object or idea to some extent has me in its power. If I freely give it away, I release myself from that bond, and in a sense come fully to own it. So the more I give, the more I have, until, when I have given everything, all possessions, all fixed views and ideas, the universe is mine.

• Thinking that building myself a coffin from planks of fragrant macrocarpa would bring a spark to my practice. As I measured and cut, dowelled and sanded the planks, I found myself visualizing my body at home in its wooden box. A strange sense of peace pervaded me, the peace of facing no more responsibility or worry. Then unease, leading to understanding. What was welling up through all my 'spiritual' beliefs was what Buddhists call the 'false view of nihilism', the belief that consciousness ends with the death of the body. No more worries, just annihilation. Acquiring new beliefs can be so much easier than off-loading the old ones! The coffin, a handsome piece of furniture, fitted with temporary shelves, was installed at the head of my bed to store my books and to remind me that life is too brief to forgive procrastination.

• The weekly meeting of the men's chapter – joining with six other members of the Order to discuss matters related to our spiritual path. Vimalajyoti's 'I have a little idea I'd like to try,' meeting general assent, he asked us to sit quiet and still for a few minutes, then to take ourselves in imagination to the most positive event in our lives. Immediately, to my surprise, I found myself in the stupa at Guhyaloka, reliving the ceremony in which I was given my name and the Green Tara practice. From a great distance came Vimalajyoti's voice, 'Now, keeping that positivity, take yourself to your death bed. Note how you are feeling, who is with you, and how you respond to them.' I was lying peacefully on a bed in a state of joyful anticipation. With me were two Order members, Prajnalila (formerly Diane) and a man I could not identify. Having overcome their attachment, both were silently assuring me that they were OK, and encouraging me to move on. A sudden fear: what if a relative arrived who had not overcome attachment, so tried to hold me back? I could not handle that. I would have to ask them to leave. Again the voice from far away, 'Go back a year. You have a year to live. What do you need to do in that year?' The answer came without hesitation. 'Deepen my relationship with Tara, that's all I need to do.' A panicky voice from the shadow of Provider, 'But what about all the teaching and other important things you do?' And an answering voice, this time from Tara, 'Yes, they are important, but only as aspects of your relationship with me.'

• Sitting on a clifftop at Kawau watching the breeze-blown wavelets chasing each other past the reef below. Noticing for the first time that a wave is not a 'thing' that runs from horizon to horizon. Each wave rises then falls away, while another rises in the trough behind it. There is no such thing as a wave – there is only coming to be and passing away – which illustrates one of the most basic of all Buddhist teachings, 'All things arise from conditions; when the conditions change, the phenomenon changes.' So no thing has permanent identity. Every thing, every event, arises dependent on conditions, none of which is itself permanent. All existence is process. I am process. I have no fixed identity, no fixed self. Since I am constant change, my task on the spiritual path is not to change myself but to influence the change that is constant and inevitable. Further, to try to resist change is like Canute and the tide – it can only lead to failure.

• Vessantara, a visiting teacher from England, leading a workshop on the Warrior, took me, along with a roomful of others, in a guided mediation through our personal fears towards a state of fearlessness. A moment, a split second, of total fearlessness, and with it the realization that all that stood between me and Enlightenment was the fear of loss of my self-image. Fearful enough, since it meant the death of my identity, painstakingly built up over so many years, if not many lifetimes. Yet it was another demon identified, named, and to a degree disempowered.

So have the years of practice rolled on, long periods of apparently little happening punctuated by sparks of insight into the way things really are. In fact life in the city, with its multitude of activities and distractions, became mostly 'just pressing on with practice'. Most of the sparks happened, and still happen, during solitary retreats (chapter 30).

A word of explanation about demons. In the sense in which most Buddhists use the term, a demon is an embodiment of a mind state, generally unconscious, that limits one's progress on the spiritual path. The art of managing a demon is, first, to recognize and acknowledge it as part of oneself, then to make friends with it. Demons are essentially lonely, lost, and rejected, so they respond enthusiastically to any suggestion of friendship. I first met this method of sorting out the murky depths of one's mind in 1989 at a retreat at Padmaloka in Norfolk. The retreat was led by Aloka, a man deeply familiar with this sort of mythology. He looked the part, fortyish, long black hair showing the first streaks of grey, friendly smile displaying a missing upper incisor, black shirt emblazoned with a white skull, and a selection of bones worn as pendants. I never saw him with any other clothes or ornaments. At our first meeting in the shrine room he suggested that we make small shrines in front of the main one, at which to make offerings to our personal demons. Since all this was somewhat foreign to a suburban doctor approaching retirement, I questioned whether it was appropriate for me to be involved with it. Aloka listened sympathetically to my protest, and settled the argument with, 'If they won't come to the party you can't transform them, can you?' Feeling somewhat foolish – being a stranger in a foreign land reduced the embarrassment a little – I made a shrine at which I dutifully offered the demons chocolate biscuits, since I had no trace of an idea who or what they were. During the next week or two there came, to my surprise, and sometimes distress, pride, doubt, covetousness, even the elusive anger, and many more, crowding into my consciousness. They were lured more, I supposed, by the increasing sincerity with which I made my offerings than by the chocolate biscuits. And to varying extents they were transformed by the atmosphere of the retreat into being not only less obstructive but even supportive of my efforts. By the time we came to the final ritual of casting written confessions into a bonfire while circumambulating it under the full moon, chanting Sanskrit mantras the while – though still wondering what my patients would have thought of such a carry-on – I had no doubts about the effectiveness of the practice.

In Buddhist literature there are many accounts of sages transforming demons into willing servants by befriending them. It could be said that the power a demon has over one comes only from one's resistance to it. As soon as one recognizes, acknowledges, and welcomes the demon, its power to harm is lost. Although there are references to this truth in Western mythology, for example the tale of Rumpelstiltskin, its full understanding waited for millennia until Freud and the school of psychoanalysis proclaimed it as new knowledge.

Yet another transforming event from those few years. June 1996 saw me back at Padmaloka attending my third reunion of the men with whom I had been ordained (I missed the retreat in 1994). When I poured out my heart to Subhuti, telling him about the battles I was having with addictive activity, he quite uncharacteristically became directive. 'Go home and be your age,' he told me. 'Do what you can do better than most because of your experience of life, and don't waste your time doing what younger men can do better. Give up administration and everything else you can offload. Make *kalyana mitrata* [spiritual friendship] the basis of your practice. To do your job of kalyana mitra you need to be well in touch with your going for refuge [spiritual commitment] and with your life's experience. Set up the conditions in which you can meet Tara, reflect on the Dharma and your experience, and be available to whoever wants to meet you.' Such simple advice, but it hit me like a ton of bricks, both because it was so obviously what I needed to do and because Subhuti had never before given me direct advice.

'Reflect on the Dharma.' Until I met Buddhist practice, the art of reflection was something quite unknown to me. From the questions I hear in discussion groups, I have come to believe it is just as much of a stranger to many others. A word about this gentle but surprisingly effective practice. For me, thinking – problem solving, planning, manipulating ideas – is a conscious, directed process, apparently (but not truly) free from emotional involvement, located somewhere behind the eyes. Meditation is a relatively spontaneous, undirected process, located somewhere in the region of the heart, and more obviously associated with emotion. Thinking is profoundly influenced by personal likes and dislikes, prejudices, and attitudes; meditation becomes less so as concentration develops. Thinking leads to answers; meditation to insights. Reflection, for me, happens halfway between thought and meditation, somewhere around the level of the throat. It begins when the mind is sufficiently calmed to have discarded much of its chatter, but not to the point of disappearance of directed thought. It is less deliberate than problem solving, but still held to a chosen topic and guided towards understanding. And for me, reflection is the process that unravels tangles, arranges concepts, feelings, and emotions into coherent patterns, and assimilates conclusions into the pre-existing frameworks of understanding.

A diary entry about a year later tells of the sort of reflections that came to mind.

Generosity is having time for people while maintaining equanimity through awareness of my own needs, and keeping firmly in touch with plan and purpose.

And a short while later:

I can support others in what they do, just by being around and sharing experience. Just being around is not being useless.

Then, as an afterthought:

It's OK to be useless!

This last would have been blasphemy only a few years earlier. What it meant, of course, was that being 'useless' gave me the space to be aware of myself, of other people, of the world, and even of the nature of Reality, while being busy was to blind myself to much of that. A further reflection of some time later:

> What Subhuti was pointing me to, the Wise Old Man, is certainly a far call from where I am now. But it's a much further call from where I was a year ago. Who is the Wise Old Man? To the world he is Mentor. He is the embodiment of wisdom, born of experience. He sees all without reacting, he loves all because he has transcended self-view, he achieves all because his action is spontaneous and appropriate, a response to what is. In that sense he 'does his duty'. He meets the needs of the situation. Subjectively, the Wise Old Man is content. He appreciates and enjoys reality. He no longer needs to fight for his own needs. He has transcended conflict and can enjoy the beauty of reality with a mind at peace. He responds to the joys and sorrows of others with clear, pure empathy – a perfect blend of understanding and love. He feels compassion and sympathetic joy appropriately, because he has transcended self-pity and elation. Yes, the Wise Old Man is a long way from where I am now, but I can experience him in imagination, which is new, so rejoice in the distance travelled so far.

I would have found these years difficult and exciting enough without the adventures I had with surgeons plying their craft on my unwilling body. The first was the repair of an innocent-looking hernia that had begun to bulge through the scar left from the 1991 surgery. That turned out to be a major exercise involving the insertion of a piece of synthetic fabric in my upper belly wall. Patching living tissue with an inert material more commonly used for making raincoats, I found quite distasteful. However, when I voiced this concern to my friendly surgeon, he could only comment, 'Sorry about that. I ran out of bits of you to patch up the holes,' and with that I had to be content. It took me all of a year to learn to live with the tugging and pulling of an inelastic foreign body in my very elastic abdominal wall without piling the pain of hatred for the intrusive thing on to the physical discomfort.

No sooner had I come to terms with that, than I caught the toe of my sandal on the edge of the jetty while going ashore from the Kawau ferry, and fell heavily on my right side. A quick survey showed bruises and abrasions, and, yes, some weakness of the right shoulder, but no serious injury. However, the next six months, which included the 1996 trip to England, saw the development of progressively intolerable pain in the shoulder. The next friendly surgeon, this time a specialist in shoulder injuries, having completed the necessary examinations and technical investigations, gave me the verdict. 'Ruptured rotator cuff and impingement of humerus on acromion. I'll need to chop some off the acromion, patch the hole, and repair the tendons. Six weeks in a sling and six months mobilizing. Should be OK for light work after that.' He was not a man to waste words. The lack of enthusiasm with which I received this news was irrelevant. I needed to be free of constant pain even at the cost of some horrid surgery and the prospect of long term limitation. In the event, although the surgery and immediate after-effects were as unpleasant as predicted, recovery was much quicker and more complete than I had been led to expect. For the next six years my body was as good a new, until another minor injury triggered the whole unhappy train of events again: months of increasing pain in the shoulder, even more extensive repairs, and slow return of function. With all due respect (some of my best friends are surgeons), may my future association with surgeons be on any business other than their gruesome art.

As the years rolled by, the possibility of attaining the still, contemplative life while living in the city was slipping away over the horizon. I was living an enjoyable and useful life for which I was grateful to the Dharma and all it gave me, but I wanted more. I wanted to expand awareness and love beyond the restrictions of ordinary experience. I needed more time relatively free from distraction. The truth that Subhuti had tried to impress on me was beginning to penetrate. I could offer more to the world as a 'friend in the good life' than as a man busily getting things done. So arose the habit of escaping to be alone on Kawau Island for a few days or even a few weeks whenever I could. Although I returned from these solitary retreats refreshed and inspired, always with some new understanding to pass on, the nagging little voice followed me for years. 'Bit of a shirker, aren't you, leaving the others to do the work while you sit on your bum on an island.' ('Shirker' was probably the worst insult my father could have offered to any man.)

The balance was too precarious to last. The fact was that the Kawau cottage was not really suited to intense spiritual practice. Still populated by ghosts of children as well as a few from my own younger self, occupied in competition with other family members, and too close to Auckland to escape the pressure of increasing population, it was no longer the peaceful haven that I needed. Fortunately, by the time I came to casting about for an alternative refuge, a solitary retreat hut had been built on our land, later to be called Sudarshanaloka, in the Tararu Valley near Thames. So from 1996 Chetul Hut increasingly became my second home, until by the end of the millennium, not without some grief, I abandoned Kawau completely.

# 29

# ... and in the bush

'The bush' was (and is) Sudarshanaloka, a place and a project so dear to my heart that I dare to quote at some length from an article I wrote in 2001 for *Dharma Life*, a Buddhist journal published in England.

We came to the place we now call Sudarshanaloka in the southern winter of 1993.... This was our own land, rough, raw and begging to be moulded to our needs.... So many dreams, such enthusiasm, and so little understanding of what we had undertaken.... Physically, it was 85 hectares (214 acres) of steep and rugged country in the form of a long, inverted triangle straddling a steep spur rising from the junction of two streams, to lose itself in the jumble of volcanic crags that form the Coromandel Ranges. At its lowest point, between the two streams, lay a wooden farmhouse, amateur-built and unfinished. Snaking up the central ridge, three kilometres of clay road rose 200 metres and then disappeared into the forest beyond the boundary. None of us knew quite where the boundary was. We still don't. Since we are surrounded by forest park, it isn't important.

This was a land ... carved down the ages by water from mountains thrown up by volcanic fire. Overwhelming beauty, staggering potential already being realized in excited imagination. And yet, even the most pragmatic of us could not escape a sense of brooding darkness, a feeling of resistance to our entry, of being received with resignation rather than welcome. In a clearing at the end of the old forestry road, the crown of a once-noble kauri tree lay charred and forlorn, its great limbs amputated, forty metres from the stump on which a century ago its trunk (too valued by man to survive) had stood. Remnants of old forestry roads leading to rotting stumps hiding their grief under masses of ferns. Here and there stood a dying rata tree whose only crime was to grow leaves favoured as food by the alien brush-tailed possum.... And on the ground, the way of a passing goat was marked by the occasional broken sapling and a disturbing absence of the seedlings that will fill gaps created when ancient trees fall. The New Zealand forest, with no experience of grazing or browsing mammals until recent centuries, is defenceless against them. Alien weeds grew where native growth had been cleared: European gorse, English ragwort, Australian wattle, and Scottish thistles. Beneath the ground lay miles of tunnels from which enormous quantities of gold-bearing quartz had been dug with hammer and chisel, pick and shovel, by men working and living in indescribably squalid conditions. And there were the scars of a century ago when the last millable timber had been removed and much of the valley burnt to prepare for the hopeless attempt to establish pasture for sheep. Aided by man, fire had reclaimed its own; and the steep lands had slumped in the rains that followed, until manuka scrub clothed its nakedness, and the forest slowly reasserted itself.

So that was where I went to 'soothe the savage breast' in the peace and beauty of the bush. And that was where Satyananda, the guiding force behind the Tararu project, built Chetul Hut. Since I cannot now reclaim the inspiration that gave rise to an article I wrote at the time for the local sangha, I quote again:

Satyananda showed me where he thought the first hut should be. I thought the access was too difficult and the big trees crowding in too much – but he went ahead anyway…. The last 150 metres of the approach was (and still is) a precipitous ridge down which every last plank, nail, and section of floor had to be carried. And of course everything was done by hand. Even if he'd had the luxury of a power tool there was (and is) no power apart from manpower.

After all that, what do we have? We have a place of elegant simplicity, with just enough concessions to luxury to remove the distractions of inconvenience and discomfort. Yet being free of some city 'necessities' like hot water, flush toilet, and mains power to drive the hair dryer, it helps us to become aware of some of our habitual attachments. Chetul Hut is in the elements and of the elements. Its builders brought enough foreign materials and ideas to let its occupants live in the elements

– and no more. They left behind nothing that would distract the mind from simplicity, beauty, and the truth that emerges from them....

Chetul Hut belongs to Green Tara, nestled as it is in the bush that is Green Tara's realm. The infinite variety of greens, from the majestic rata to the east, through the rewarewa and mamaku to the north, to the delicate koromiko peeping out from under the western deck, each in its way evokes and pays homage to Tara. The garden of mingimingi and mapou, of flax bowing to the breeze, of humble hebe with its variations on tiny, pale flowers, and red-spotted toru lovingly gathered from remote places in the bush, all brought together to beautify the already beautiful, is witness to many acts of devotion to Tara. The wind in the trees, the ever-present song of the stream, the pervading scent of decaying leaves on the forest floor, and the subtle perfumes of leaves and tiny forest flowers, the trilling warbler and golden-voiced bellbird, the kereru swooping, stalling, and tumbling in its nuptial flight, even the nocturnal rat scampering to and from its nest in the roof and testing the wire screen on the window with its sharp teeth, and the ponderous possum clumping along the deck like a weary old man seeking refuge. All the sights, smells, and sounds that together make the magical world of Chetul Hut – all are of the realm of Tara.

Since much of my time at Chetul Hut has been spent relating to Green Tara, perhaps this is the time to tell a little of the history of this relationship to date. After many years of her growth and change, even metamorphosis, I find it difficult to go back to Tara as she was when she first came into my life. Come into my life she certainly did. I have no recollection of seeking her, or even anticipating her arrival. She appeared, apparently spontaneously, there on the peak of the Mythical Mountain all those lifetimes ago, as an inner essence of Fountain.

Until that moment, my knowledge of Tara was minimal. I had read the legend of her birth from the tears of Avalokitesvara, with whom I had developed some relationship. The only picture in my mind was that of a semi-clothed princess of ancient India, in full lotus posture, and, as befits a daughter of Avalokitesvara, pure white. My response to the green woman of my meditation as she discovered her identity was of shocked disbelief. 'You can't be Tara,' I found my inner voice saying. 'Tara is white!' But from that moment I could hold no doubt that this being, as far as I could relate to her, was truly Tara.

She was as advanced a spiritual being as my imagination of that time could meet. After all, she had momentarily taken me with her into a realm beyond time and space. This was no ordinary dream symbol. This was a goddess, a being of the earth but also of the heavens, whose quality was receptivity. She was totally receptive to the presence and the needs of all beings, to whom she spoke, in their own tongue, a message of infinite love. Yet she retained a boyish figure, and with it an earthy humour, wielded with deep kindness whenever my pomposity needed puncturing. So she remained for a year or so, appearing in my meditation whenever I needed her special qualities. Under her influence I became gentler, more responsive, more appreciative, of other people and of beauty, especially natural beauty, and at the same time more aware of the response of others to me. Although I was aware of changes in my perception, I had no inclination to investigate what was happening. I was happy just to let it happen. Tara, and her influence on me, was the growth of receptivity.

After a time, Tara began to appear in my meditation in her more popular classical form, the emerald-green princess dressed in royal silks and jewels. Seated on a pale blue lotus, her left leg folded in meditation posture and her right foot stepping down from her throne, she carried her compassionate action into the midst of the suffering of the world. Her left hand was held in the gesture of fearlessness, while the right was extended, resting on her right knee, palm forward in a gesture of supreme generosity. At first, the form she appeared in seemed to be randomly chosen. As I sat down to meditate I could never guess which, if any, would appear. A pattern slowly emerged. When my need was for unquestioning receptivity, the total acceptance of mother love, Tara appeared as the soft green wood-nymph who had emerged from the body of Fountain on the mountain top. When understanding was called for, especially when an active response to suffering was needed, her form was that of the Princess, carrying in her crown the jewels of the five wisdoms of the Buddhas. The Tara of Wisdom and Compassion took over my life more and more, responding to my needs with anything from playful irreverence to glorious transcendence of all selfishness and confusion. I came to rely more and more on her guidance as she showed up my vanity and ignorance while encouraging expressions of generosity and understanding.

If Provider is working hard to close the gap between himself and Tara, so is Tara reaching out to Provider. She has no power to change him or anybody else; she can only invite, make welcome, and respond to those who meet her with faith, trust, and devotion. But she does have tricks to help her devotees, not the least of which is fascination with her overwhelming beauty. The more she can induce her followers to be aware of her, visualize her, and reflect on her qualities, the more they absorb her compassion and her insight into the nature of existence, and the more likely they are to fall in love with her, to their great benefit. I believe it is this fascination that will eventually win over Provider into give up his old identity, in fact to allow himself to die, so that he can be reborn as an aspect of Tara.

With the passing years, Tara has appeared in meditation in a bewildering variety of forms, from which it is becoming apparent that the form is irrelevant, a product of my own limited mind. Behind the form is a being whose true reality is so far beyond my imagination that without an intermediary to guide my perception I would be unable to make any contact with the ultimate at all. So whether Tara is mostly a projection of my needs, my reaching out to Reality, or whether she is Reality reaching out to me, is again irrelevant, since ultimately there is no difference. I am not separate from Reality, nor is Reality outside me. What matters is that this form of practice works for me. It helps me to penetrate the depths of my being and to relate to whatever is ultimate in existence, especially to expand my awareness of, and response to, the needs of all beings, including myself.

In the bush, there is time for other practices that also work for me. When there is no urgency, no need to finish a book or master a certain teaching before the next class, studying the word of the Buddha and recent commentaries on it can be a great joy. The urge to simplicity, and reluctance to carry more than absolutely necessary over the crazy little track to the hut, usually limit my study material to one book, a book to be read slowly, savoured, and reflected upon at length. Somewhere in my pack there are diaries, records of reflections from the last two or three retreats, to remind me where my thinking had reached and to start new thoughts rolling. And, of course, new diaries to be written, partly for the future, but mainly, through the process of writing, to slow the chaotic mind and gently restrain it to a stream of reflection instead of allowing it to perform like a monkey in a fig tree.

I mention thoughts, but the energy behind these activities is greater than thoughts. It arises from interaction with the things that stir the heart to appreciation, joy, and love. Beginning with opening the heart to the beauty of mountain, forest, and all they contain, discovering and befriending the spirits of the land, and expanding the devotion to one's highest ideals. Rituals evolve to develop these myths and bring them more clearly into awareness. Rituals to bring one closer to the energies of nature, usually performed in the presence of 'a noble puriri tree whose dense, evergreen foliage cast so deep a shade that little grew in the filtered, green light beneath it. Under its protection was a natural clearing some 25 metres across, carpeted with dead leaves and surrounded by a wall of tree ferns and hanging vines. A place of peace and reverence, whose silence was disturbed only by the song of the many birds that gathered to feast on the tree's abundant berries. This was more than just a forest tree. Here was a presence that evoked from all who encountered it responses of respect, reverence and even a sense of the sacred.' (From the *Dharma Life* article previously quoted.)

To open these rituals I often use lines I wrote to greet the spirits of the land in a public dedication:

We come to you in reverence and friendship.
We ask your help, that
Together we may rebuild your land and forest,
Together we may grow in love and wisdom,
Together we may find freedom from all
That binds us to sorrow and suffering.

These rituals fan the embers of devotion to wisdom and compassion, in the form of Tara or any of a multitude of other archetypal figures, into a living flame whose energy carries me forward in my quest. They take me to the stupa, an imposing seven-metre-high reliquary of white concrete, growing from a clearing in the forest, which symbolizes the path to Enlightenment. Here is the energy of the Dharma that we brought to the land.

And this brings me to the myth of Sudarshanaloka itself, which to me is the destruction of the natural state of the land by our well-meaning but misguided ancestors, its slow regeneration, and now our joining with it in partnership to restore it to its former grandeur. For me, this spells out the myth of my own life, from the violence and

174

killing that was part of my early life on a country hill-farm, through the phase of natural restoration, to active participation in the evolution of compassion and understanding. I share with the land, and all it supports, an empathy and joyful participation in the creative process of restoration and the strive towards wholeness.

According to Buddhism, body and mind are aspects of the same reality, to be treated with the same consideration and reverence. So restoration of the body is an important part of these bush retreats. Besides which, it is fun. Most days see me walking the bush tracks, machete and secateurs slung over my shoulder, to trim the invading jungle. Perhaps it takes only half an hour to clear the mind and revive the sluggish body; perhaps it is a relatively major excursion to explore a rocky river or a precipitous crag, to revel in wild beauty and to enjoy the weariness of a well-exercised body. As the years pass, these explorations become less adventurous until, with some regret, some have been abandoned. One major peak, which challenged strength and courage and gave a commanding view of the country from Rangitoto to the central Waikato, I climbed 'for the last time' on three successive summer retreats. Long after the final 'last time' I could still feel the stir of challenge when I caught sight of its towering form from a gentler track. And there is always gardening, and minor maintenance work on Chetul Hut, even though it is only a single room of eighteen square metres.

In recent years I have spent up to three months of each year alone in the bush. As with suburban medical practice, retreats in the bush have their more exciting moments. One of my more adventurous habits is to explore old tracks, especially overgrown forestry roads of a century ago. These have a habit of leading one deep into uncharted territory only to disappear, perhaps into a swamp, or more frequently to be interrupted by a landslide, and stubbornly refuse to reappear. I have been enticed many times into dense jungle, to be deserted in an impenetrable tangle of supple-jack, bush-lawyer, and a tough, stringy vine whose name I have never known but whose refusal to yield to machete or secateurs I have come to know very well.

On one such occasion, having struggled for an hour or more through increasingly dense undergrowth before losing the track, I elected to turn uphill to find a main track that I was sure was no more than half an hour away. An hour or two later – time was no longer relevant – I found myself crawling under barriers of vines too dense to cut, hungry, thirsty, weary, and, although not doubting that I was still on course for my track, seriously doubting whether I had the endurance to make it back to the haven of the hut. There was now no question of turning back. I had in my pack both my EPIRB (Emergency Position Indicating Radio Beacon) that I had carried for years in the sure knowledge that I would never use it, and my mobile phone, but one was only for life-threatening emergencies and the other was out of range of a signal. With growing desperation I struggled on through clinging undergrowth, until, too exhausted for caution, I blundered over a small bank to land face down on my track, not twenty minutes from home.

Another adventurous day saw me exploring a creek that formed a remote part of the boundary of our property. This time I was not lost. When I met the waterfall I knew I was no more than ten minutes from a familiar track – but I had travelled two laborious hours to this point and was reluctant to turn back. The waterfall was no more than four metres high and was well covered at its edge with dracophyllum which promised a good hold. I had reached the top and was reaching for a more substantial hand-hold when the stem in my left hand parted from the ground. As my right hand sensed the roots to which it was clutching giving way one by one, the wildly groping left clamped on to a single supple-jack vine that would have been just out of reach had I not been spurred by desperation, allowing me to haul myself to safety. Of course I promised myself I would not climb another vertical bank with only the weak-rooted dracophyllum to hang on to, but the bush is clever at presenting other hazards.

Another clear, sunny day saw me carefully picking my way over the rocks in a riverbed when a foot slipped and I fell. It was not long after the second operation on my right shoulder – and I was falling to my right. In the second or so of free fall, I checked which bones and ligaments were most vulnerable, how best to protect them, and twisted my body to present the most shock-resistant part of my anatomy to the unsympathetic rocks. When I later analysed this gymnastic feat I was amazed at the speed with which the mind and body can respond to a fearful emergency.

# 30

# growing old

There's no doubt that I'm getting old. The body becomes increasingly like the eighty-year-old Buddha's description, 'an old cart tied together with straps'. My own analogy is of a high-mileage car showing the marks of past repairs, at risk of failure of any of its multitude of parts, but still functioning tolerably well if not asked to go beyond its limits.

The lifestyle I've chosen does nothing to soften the effects of ageing. For fourteen years I have found myself twenty to forty years older than nearly everybody with whom I have lived, meditated, studied, and worked. Not only does this highlight my waning powers, but it makes it more difficult to grow out of overactivity. It is difficult to grow old gracefully when surrounded by energetic younger men. However, the age gap is not all bad. In recent years only one close friend of mine has died. Contrast the experience of Mary Rose, who in the year preceding her death attended the funerals of three friends in one fortnight.

I become more aware of the shrinking of what I call the working reserve. The concept first came to me nearly half a century ago when I was travelling considerably over the speed limit as a passenger in Ralph's new Jaguar, heading for Wellington and the ship to England.

'Why do you have a car,' I asked him, 'that will do 130 miles an hour when the law and the roads limit you to 70?'

'If I drive at 70 in a car that will only do 80, there's no reserve for comfort or safety,' he told me. 'This car has plenty of both at this speed.'

At that moment, we came upon a cow ambling across the road. We came to a stop with most of a car length to spare. Nobody had thought about seat belts in those days. As I peeled myself off the windscreen I was moved to agree with him.

This concept of working reserve followed me right through my medical career. The stress my patients could tolerate before becoming dysfunctional was a measure of their working reserve. As maximum capacity diminished with age or other impairment, this reserve shrank until, at the point at which it faded out altogether, disability appeared without any extra stress. A special case was what I used to call compensated disability, of which the classic example was a friend with a leaking heart valve, who lived an apparently normal life until a mild chest infection threw him into crippling heart failure. As I grow older I sometimes feel myself perilously close to the point of decompensation of one function or another. There is some comfort in the fact that when disability does appear, it might take only a small nudge to tip the balance back to normal function. If I approach an evening study group aware of sluggish thought processes and find myself groping for words, the small dose of adrenaline generated by a difficult question dramatically (if temporarily) corrects the defect. So reliable is this effect that I am given to dropping a provocative remark early in the evening to stir up some controversy and kick start my tardy brain.

On one retreat arose the question: why, as I grow older, do I become more prone to anxiety? As I sat allowing the question to sink in, the answer slowly emerged. Because my strength has been dominant, competitive, wilful, backed by reserves of confidence and energy. I have been able through my own power to meet whatever arises. Now that power is fading, and with it confidence in my ability to meet what the world turns up. My father's teaching that led me to think 'if I'm the most capable person here to meet the situation I'll do my best, and if that's not good enough, so be it,' is no longer enough.

What is the threat if I can no longer cope as I could in the past? A large part of it is 'They will see. They will know I'm losing it. They will scorn me and not respect me any more.' It seems very important to keep command of the situation sufficiently to know what I should give up before I undertake what I can no longer do. It is also important to trust a friend to help me, to point out to me that it is time I gave that task to somebody else or left it undone.

How to manage anxiety if I become aware of it? One way is to project it into a form of a little demon, then set about making friends with it. Perhaps this method is available only to those who visualize easily, but in my experience it is much easier and more effective to relate to a mischievous little demon than to the vague sensation of anxiety. Another method I often use for anxiety, or any other uncomfortable emotion, is to concentrate on its physical properties. Where do I feel it? Exactly what do I feel? Is it heavy or light? Hot or cold? Does it have a colour? And so on. This achieves a number of things. First, it draws me away from any tendency to react to the anxiety with aversion, which would only add one discomfort to another. Then it deepens my awareness of what is actually happening in my present experience, which is a positive state that strengthens threatened confidence. With practice, the physical accompaniments of anxiety (or other emotion) can become apparent before the emotion is felt, and act as a warning. For me, it is tightening of the scalp that warns me to attend to the situation before it gets on top of me.

Of course, all functions slow down together. I move and think more slowly, tire more quickly, sleep less soundly, find words less reliably, and hear less acutely in the higher frequencies where reside many of the consonants that make speech intelligible. But there is no need to detail exhaustively such common experience. The positive aspects of ageing are less frequently reported. From a combination of good fortune and hard work I could afford to stop earning money at the age of sixty and be free to apply myself to the Buddhist path full time. Had this not been so, starting as late in life as I did, I would certainly not have made the progress I have so far achieved.

What progress have I made? One innocent young man's question in a study group was, 'How has twenty years of being a Buddhist changed you?' I found myself deluged with new questions, reflections, insights, and emotional responses. How has seventy-four years of being a human being changed me? How much of the profound change of the last twenty years can I attribute to my being a Buddhist? Are all the changes progress, or have I been drifting sideways or slipping backwards? Who is it that changes? Who am I?

The most tangible change is that not only am I happier and more fulfilled, but my enjoyment of life continues to grow. The satisfaction of life as a family doctor was underlain by the knowledge that it was not and could not be enough. In no way did it reach the causes of happiness or the purpose of life. So where is true satisfaction to be found? Following the Buddha's famous formula, which led to his description of the chain of causation that governs human life, 'In dependence on what did this experience arise?' Happiness arises in dependence on, among other things, awareness and love. As I commented to the young man whose question started these reflections, 'There's a limit to how much fun you can have if you don't really know you are having it!' I had not been meditating long before I discovered that awareness is a strongly positive state. The more deeply I am aware of what I am experiencing at this moment, the more positive I feel, even if the experience is one of the less acceptable emotions like anger or jealousy, or even physical pain. I could theorize about this, but the proof lies in a term applied in classical literature to the whole of the Buddha's teaching, *ehipassiko*, meaning 'come and see'.

But how does love come into this? From deepening awareness of myself and the world about me, arises acceptance that this is who I am, this is how things are, and that's OK. Far from being a state of apathy, this is a recognition of where I am starting from to make the changes that I see are necessary. I begin to see myself and other people less and less according to my own reactions, so profoundly coloured by prejudice and conditioning, and increasingly as we really are. It is now only a short step to appreciation and enjoyment of self and other, to empathy, and, in short, to love. I should point out that what I am calling love is quite different from the romantic love so dear to Shakespeare and Hollywood, in which true appreciation of the beloved is so often swamped by cleverly concealed projection and seeking what we desire.

For all its positivity, deepening my awareness does bring some difficulties. The more aware I become, the more little insights into the nature of existence tend to pop up. They are usually no more than pinholes in the veils that screen me from Reality, but each spark of light diffuses through the whole of my previous understanding, bringing it just a tiny bit more to life. However, each small step is inclined to open new landscapes littered with attitudes and views that limit progress and need clearing away. Far from being discouraging, this continuing discovery of more work to be done is an inspiration and a challenge. I do confess, though, that there have been times in the early stages of the journey when I wondered if I were going backwards.

A teaching of many years ago, whose truth is still unfolding, is that all aspects of spiritual growth have two stages. First comes a measure of conceptual understanding of a truth, then, as that soaks into my being, the act of changing myself in the light of that understanding. The difficulty is that, since the initial understandings come so much more readily than the changes, visible deficiencies tend to pile up on each other to await attention. One consequence of this is that as I grow older I have less and less interest in acquiring new knowledge. I don't expect to live long enough to assimilate, integrate, and bring action to everything I already know. Since acquiring knowledge becomes more difficult with each passing year, I am relieved to find it becoming less and less necessary. In passing, the increasing difficulty in learning new facts proceeds in parallel with difficulties in remembering what I have learned. It is as though access to the memory bank is closing down, progressively obstructing the processes of squeezing things in and winkling them out. Given time, patience, and effort, both processes still function, albeit somewhat unreliably.

It is commonly believed that resistance to change increases with the passing years. In the absence of growing awareness, this may well be true, but my experience is that as my contact with the Buddha's teaching deepens, I am more ready to face change. Not that this is, or ever will be, easy. Another teaching I met long ago is that all misery comes from trying to make permanent that which is impermanent, trying to convince myself that passing states of mind, events, and objects (including myself) are fixed, permanent, and can bring security and satisfaction, instead of enjoying each moment as it passes. I become more able to accept that attempting to fix anything in time or place is only to promote an illusion. Just as my car wears out, my old views become outdated, my children grow up and go to live on the other side of the world, my old body is prone to aches and pains, and death becomes more of a reality. All this is OK, to be acknowledged as the way things are. If there is pain, that is suffering enough without my piling misery on top of it by allowing myself to develop hatred for it. I have known these things for many years, with knowledge that resides behind my eyes. This knowledge now comes to rest more in my heart, slowly infiltrating itself into my being, bringing with it a measure of peace and equanimity.

Reflection on old age inevitably leads to thoughts about approaching death. In chapter 15 I commented on death and speculated a little on what might happen to the stream of consciousness that I regard as myself when the body dies. That was speculation, interesting to me since I have now lived something between eighty-five and ninety-nine percent of this life, but not touching the heart's experience. What is my heart's reaction to death? Imagining the world continuing without me rouses little response. No longer being present to enjoy the many things I now enjoy is of little concern – provided I am not aware of it. But as Hamlet so poignantly observed, 'To sleep: perchance to dream'. There is no reason to suppose that awareness and responsibility for decisions disappear at the same time as the body. What undoubtedly does disappear is the protection from reality that the physical body gives me. So my concern is that when I am freed from all restrictions and faced with unlimited opportunity for spiritual growth, I will let it slip by because of ignorance and fear. The obvious answer is to spur myself to greater effort in my practice while I have a relatively sound body and mind within which to do it. The deeper my contact with the way things are, the less unfamiliar will be the *bardo* (the 'in-between' place, in this case between one life and the next) when I meet it. Yet even as the years separating me from the funeral pyre crumble away, I continue to let much of my time be filled with the trivialities of daily life. The conclusion is inescapable: in the depth of my being I still cling to some belief that I will live for ever. May I live long enough to discard that illusion!

The windhorse symbolizes the energy of the Enlightened mind carrying the truth of the Buddha's teachings to all corners of the world. On its back the windhorse bears three jewels: a brilliant gold jewel represents the Buddha, the ideal of Enlightenment, a sparkling blue jewel represents the teachings of the Buddha, the Dharma, and a glowing red jewel, the community of the Buddha's enlightened followers, the Sangha. Windhorse Publications, through the medium of books, similarly takes these three jewels out to the world.

Windhorse Publications is a Buddhist publishing house, staffed by practising Buddhists. We place great emphasis on producing books of high quality, accessible and relevant to those interested in Buddhism at whatever level. Drawing on the whole range of the Buddhist tradition, our books include translations of traditional texts, commentaries, books that make links with Western culture and ways of life, biographies of Buddhists, and works on meditation.

As a charitable institution we welcome donations to help us continue our work. We also welcome manuscripts on aspects of Buddhism or meditation. For orders and catalogues log on to www.windhorsepublications.com or contact:

Windhorse Publications
11 Park Road
Birmingham
B13 8AB
UK

Consortium
1045 Westgate Drive
St Paul MN 55114
USA

Windhorse Books
PO Box 574
Newtown NSW 2042
Australia

Windhorse Publications is an arm of the Friends of the Western Buddhist Order, which has more than sixty centres on four continents. Through these centres, members of the Western Buddhist Order offer regular programmes of events for the general public and for more experienced students. These include meditation classes, public talks, study on Buddhist themes and texts, and bodywork classes such as t'ai chi, yoga, and massage. The FWBO also runs several retreat centres and the Karuna Trust, a fundraising charity that supports social welfare projects in the slums and villages of India.

Many FWBO centres have residential spiritual communities and ethical businesses associated with them. Arts activities are encouraged too, as is the development of strong bonds of friendship between people who share the same ideals. In this way the FWBO is developing a unique approach to Buddhism, not simply as a set of techniques, but as a creatively directed way of life for people living in the modern world.

If you would like more information about the FWBO please visit the website at www.fwbo.org or write to:

London Buddhist Centre
51 Roman Road
London
E2 0HU
UK

Aryaloka
14 Heartwood Circle
Newmarket NH 03857
USA

Sydney Buddhist Centre
24 Enmore Road
Sydney NSW 2042
Australia

# ALSO FROM WINDHORSE PUBLICATIONS

## CHANGE YOUR MIND:
### A practical guide to Buddhist meditation
by Paramananda

This best-selling and thorough guide to meditation is based on traditional material but written in a light and modern style. Colourfully illustrated with anecdotes and tips from the author's experience as a meditator and teacher, it also offers refreshing inspiration to seasoned meditators.

Buddhism is based on the truth that, with effort, we can change the way we are. But how? Among the many methods Buddhism has to offer, meditation is the most direct. It is the art of getting to know one's own mind and learning to encourage what is best in us. *Change Your Mind* is a wonderful place to start.

208 pages, b/w photographs
ISBN 1 899579 75 3
£9.99/$13.95/€13.95

## PRINCIPLES OF BUDDHISM
by Kulananda

Buddhism is one of the most popular religions of today – its teachings on kindness, simplicity, and interconnectedness are attracting many people disenchanted with the world's all-pervading consumerism.

This simple guide holds the essential teachings and methods of practice to help bring these qualities alive. Going back to the roots of Buddhism, it highlights and explains:

- the central ideas and beliefs of Buddhism
- karma and rebirth
- meditation
- Buddhism in the world today

The author, Kulananda, a practising Buddhist for over thirty years, shows us how this approach to life can make a real difference to us and our capacity to grow clearer, wiser, and happier.

160 pages
ISBN 1 899579 59 1
£5.99/$8.95/€8.95

**WHAT IS THE DHARMA?**
The essential teachings of the Buddha
by Sangharakshita

To walk in the footsteps of the Buddha we need a clear and thorough guide to the essential principles of Buddhism. Whether we have just begun our journey or are a practitioner with more experience, *What is the Dharma?* is an indispensable exploration of the Buddha's teachings as found in the main Buddhist traditions.

Constantly returning to the question 'How can this help me?' Sangharakshita examines a variety of fundamental principles, including: karma and rebirth, nirvana and shunyata, conditioned co-production, impermanence, unsatisfactoriness and insubstantiality, ethics, meditation, and wisdom.

The result is a refreshing, unsettling, and inspiring book that lays before us the essential Dharma – timeless and universal.

272 pages
ISBN 1 899579 01 X
£9.99/$16.95/€16.95

**DIPA MA:**
The life and legacy of a Buddhist master
by Amy Schmidt

*This book, like Dipa Ma, is simple, straightforward and powerful.*
**Alice Walker**, author of *The Color Purple*

*An inspiring and beautiful book about one of our most beloved elders, a modern Buddhist saint.*          **Jack Kornfield**, author of *After the Ecstasy the Laundry*

Read the life story and spiritual teachings of Dipa Ma, a major figure in contemporary Buddhism. She was the teacher of such well-respected western Buddhists as Jack Kornfield, Sharon Salzberg, Joseph Goldstein, Alice Walker and Sylvia Boorstein, among others.

An accomplished yogi, she was an inspired teacher and a devoted mother and grandmother. A woman who found great freedom through profound levels of insight and one who exemplified in her every action immense kindness, generosity, and mindfulness.

Foreword by Sharon Salzberg
Introduction by Joseph Goldstein
Afterword by Jack Kornfield

176 pages
ISBN 1 899579 73 7
£9.99/$15.95/€15.95
*This edition is not available in North America*

## DETOX YOUR HEART

by Valerie Mason-John

*Passes on the wisdom of hard experience and shows there is a way to get yourself back on track* **Jenni Murray**, BBC's Women's Hour

*Offers readers both the inspiration and the insight to work on themselves* **Christopher Titmuss**, author of *Transforming Our Terror*

*This is a book full of heart which explores with compassion the many layers of human emotions.* **Jackee Holder**, author of *Soul Purpose*

Have you ever felt angry, resentful or even revengeful? The author, Valerie Mason-John, draws on her own life, personal stories, and current work as an anger management trainer to explore why we can experience such emotions and how we can transform toxins like anger, hatred, and fear.

Our ability to love and be open is often blocked by toxins inside the heart – jealousy, hatred, anger, prejudice, fear, resentment. With short exercises drawing on Buddhist teachings that encourage pausing, connecting, feeling, and loving, *Detox Your Heart* helps us to renew and open our heart.

208 pages
ISBN 1 899579 65 6
£9.99/$13.95/€13.95


## WRITING YOUR WAY

by Manjusvara (David Keefe)

> *It's about learning how to unlock your creativity, how to let*
> *language work through you and begin dancing across the page.*

Emerging out of the Wolf at the Door writing workshops taught worldwide, *Writing Your Way* helps us to see writing as a transformative tool in our search for wholeness. Manjusvara (David Keefe) expertly guides us to the heart of writing as well as to aspects of Buddhism, with exercises that delicately weave in teachings on mindfulness and compassion, freedom and openness.

*Contains more good advice about writing than any other book I have read* **Robert Gray**, award-winning poet and creative writing teacher

*A smart, generous, imaginative, and encouraging book about writing* **Chase Twichell**, poet and editor, Ausable Press

160 pages
ISBN 1 899579 67 2
£8.99/$12.95/€12.95